Table of Contents

Introduction..i
Those Crazy Teen Age Years...............................1
The Red Hawk Experience 15
A Road Trip, That Lasted 20 Plus Years 41
Cissie Lynn "The Forgotten One".....................82
Same Song, Different Places, Different Faces 110
Ladies and Gentlemen, Tiny Tim. 120
Different Studios, Same Bullshit.....................136
The Joy of Parenthood....................................158
The Nashville Hustle, The Hillbilly Con Train .201
Back Room Deals, Smoke And Mirrors 213
Facebook and Other Things
    That Piss Me Off..228
Friends, Players and Internet Idols 244
No Big Deal, Just Stories 283
My Final Goodbye (Maybe) 316

NIGHTMARES OF THE DREAM

#2
The Encore Edition

A MUSICAL JOURNEY OF THE LIFE AND TIMES OF AWARD WINNING RECORD PRODUCER AND RECORDING ARTIST

DOC HOLIDAY

The Hard Core Facts About The Business Of Music

Nightmares of the Dream #2, The Encore Edition
A Musical Journey of the Life and Times of Award Winning
Record Producer and Recording Artist Doc Holiday
All Rights Reserved.
Copyright © 2018 Doc Holiday
v2.0

The opinions expressed in this manuscript are solely the opinions of the author and do not represent the opinions or thoughts of the publisher. The author has represented and warranted full ownership and/or legal right to publish all the materials in this book.

This book may not be reproduced, transmitted, or stored in whole or in part by any means, including graphic, electronic, or mechanical without the express written consent of the publisher except in the case of brief quotations embodied in critical articles and reviews.

Scattered Focus LLC

ISBN: 978-0-578-20072-9

Cover Photo by Doc Holiday © 2018. All rights reserved - used with permission.

PRINTED IN THE UNITED STATES OF AMERICA

Introduction

Okay, here is my second book fellow buckaroos, and to be honest with you, I probably got 20 volumes more I could write at this point, and I still would not get in all that happened along the way. But I'll try to get as many stories and events, as I can in this volume #2 of Nightmares Of The Dream.

Ya know, reading the first book, Nightmares Of The Dream was important to the readers, because, it gave you, the reader an insight to some of the crazy shit and goings on in my life. But in this second book, I jumped a little more into detail, and tell you a little bit more, of the inside stuff, and people that became a major part of what took place in my journey, through the business of music.

So, sit back and relax, this volume #2 will be a lot of new chapters, a lot of new stories and a lot of things that happen that I could not fit in the first book.

This time around, I gonna probably start in the beginning, of all the stuff that I missed in my childhood, and then go on to the artists and then moving on to the stories, along with the different events, and people who came into the picture, or should I say passed through in my life. Some being flashes, and some being memorable.

So, all the stuff that happened should be pretty cool to know about, to some of you, and those of you that don't get it, Oh well you don't know what ya missed.

I got a lot of slack, and a few lawsuits handed to me from the first volume and lost a few so called friends along the way, BUT I'm sure I'll get five times that amount from this volume. But once again, OH WELL, it is what it is. It's basically the way I saw it through my eyes, And really after all, I WAS THERE!

So sit back and relax and enjoy the read, and I hope it proves to be informative and gives you better insight, to what I went through in my lifetime, to reach this part of my success level, (If you want to call it success), and how I got there, why I got there, and more importantly, why I continue to stay there.

This second book, I will tell you right now, is loaded with personal and private conversations and events, that were never meant to be made public. But I figure at my age, with my health failing somewhat, if they were not made public, they would be lost forever. And all of it is so important, and really has to be put down in print in order to survive, and be able to explain the road, I myself traveled in order to finally reach what I was searching for, and worked so hard for, all my life.

Believe me, looking back at it. I sometimes wonder, if it was really all worth the sacrifices, hardships, pain and all the things I missed, or gave up along the way in my quest. Because in reality, when all is said and done, "Happiness depends upon ourselves. Maybe it's not about the happy ending at all, but maybe, it's all about the stories that brought us there".**So hang in there.**

Here we go!!

Those Crazy Teen Age Years

OK, well I think it's about time we get this party started. Those of you who have read my first book "Nightmares Of The Dream" already know that I hit on some of my early childhood, but I really did not get that deep into the later years as a teenager, which looking back at it now, were some pretty crazy times.

I got my Jersey drivers license and all hell broke loose. I can remember me and the guys hanging around a place called Kaylers on route 35 in Hazlet, New Jersey. It was a bar/ restaurant type thing, and it actually had an airplane mounted on the roof of the building. Well we all would go down there, and we hung out mostly in the parking lot, BUT, every once in a while, and because they had this outside type grill and counter there where they would sell hot dogs, soda and what have you. Well when the cook or counter person would take a break and leave the grill unattended, one of us would jump over the counter and grab a bunch of Jersey Hot Dogs and eat em in the parking lot. That was a huge score back then for us hoodlums.

There was a situation that happened back then, and the town of Matawan played a pretty big part in the event.

Everybody that I hung out with knew I was into the music thing, and in the first book, those of you who read the book noticed that I mentioned a lot of things that happened in my very young years, but I really didn't get to heavily involved into the later years of my teenage years.

Well let's try to correct that right now! One of the rival groups to our little town of Keyport and Hazlet was another high school in a place called Matawan, New Jersey, which was actually right down the road from our turf. It was also a huge football rivalry between Keyport High School and Matawan High School. I mean I'm talking some serious shit here. You see back then our turf was primary all Italians and Matawan was primary all Black, And I'll tell you back then, racism was alive and well in the Italian turf.

Well to make a long story short I met a guy call Ronnie Johnson, a black guy from Matawan and he had a singing group called the Six Pretenders, and I got to know him pretty good, and I would go out and listen to them sing at their house. Oh yea another thing that was really cool was they had these blue satin jackets that they wore, kinda like a gang with "The Six Pretenders" written on the back. They were all pretty tough guys but when it came to singing, they left that street toughness outside and they were awesome. They sang doo-wop and the big thing in street singers back then, was harmonizing. Hell we would hang out in a subway in New York to get that sound with a natural echo. I mean I really liked those guys both musically and personally. To put it today's terms "I was their nigger".

So anyways one night we (me and my boys) were hanging around Kaylers and we wind up having a problem with a guy, (Frankie

Huff), who came into our area from a town called Keansburg, (and that sport fans was a no no back in those days), and before you know it there's gonna be a rumble, and to be honest with you we all kinda look forward to a rumble to break the boredom, you know when your in a group like that you get to feel like your 10 feet tall and bullet proof.

The rumble was supposed to be back in the parking lot at 11 that night and there was six of us, (that was our gang), and they, (The boys from Keansburg) showed with like 15 guys. Now remember back then all rumbles always started with a lot of dialogue and insults back and forth, between the two gangs. Now I'm looking at this situation and saying to myself (We're gonna get our ass's kicked here) So I slip back into Kaylers, while my guys are talking and throwing insults at each other, and I slip into the phone booth and call up Ronnie Johnson and say, "Ronnie, I need some help, I got a situation here with some guys from Keansburg". I go back outside into the parking lot, and the leader of this group (Frankie) from Keansburg is really mouthing off, and it's all getting ready to happen now. I remember walking by one of my guys (Joe Nardelli) and telling him that I just called

Ronnie Johnson, he's on his way down, and now the insults are really flying back and forth. In the meantime Ronnie Johnson and the 6 Pretenders show up in the rear of the parking lot, and here comes six big ass black guys wearing what looks like gang colors, slipping into the back of our group. Now the leader of the guys from Keansburg was not aware of it, but all his guys that were standing behind him, notice that our gang had grown with the addition of 6 black guys, they took off creeping very slowly and quietly, and I can still remember their leader saying to me, "Jerk Off", do you think you really got a shot at me and my boys? And I can remember saying, the greatest line in the world "I don't know cause your boys just fuckin' left scum bag, and the guy turned around, and there was no one there but him. That was the end of that late night rumble, it ended without a punch being thrown. But more importantly it was the first time that white Italian kids gained respect for black guys and the rivalry between the two towns dissolved at that point in time, and that moment we were just all one.

I'll never forget that moment of coming together as one. You know music has never known a color line. There was no such thing as racism in music, between musicians, and now that night there was no color line between the guys, it was gone, if only for a moment, BUT IT WAS GONE and we all seem to come together as one. I lost track of Ronnie Johnson and often wonder what happen with those guys. I hoped they went on to bigger and better things in the music business. But the beauty of that night just goes to show you that you can take a negative and turn it into a positive real easy if you just try.

Okay getting on to my so called teen age years. We did a lot of crazy shit, when we were young, and I think the most crazy of all the years of my youth, was when I was 17 and 18 years old, and to give you just a small example of just a little of that shit.

I had a couple of good friends Fred and Bobby Frappier and we call Bobby "FLAPS", for the simple reason Bobby had a strange way of wiggling his ears. He could actually have his ears bend and flap, instead of moving up and down like most normal people who wiggled their ears did.

Anyway their father worked at an oil refinery called Hess oil New Jersey, and for some reason on the top of their garage, in an attic type room, they had bunch of huge 50 gallon drums of gasoline, and to show you how fucked up we were as kids, we would go up there, take the cap off the drums, and stick our noses and mouth inside the drum, and breath in the fumes, and sing Elvis Presley songs at the top of our lungs. We would be up there at like 2 o'clock in the morning, smelling the gas, getting high, and singing at the top of our lungs into those drums through the opening on the top. Mainly because of two reasons, One, we were getting high and Two, because when you sang the Elvis songs into the drum, it had a nice echo type sound. Well, here it is 50 plus years later and I survived. That would be just one of the events in that time period, and trust me there were plenty more.

I remember when I was 17, I had a car, it was a Plymouth Cranbrook, and it was far from being a nice car, I mean it was, at lease a car, actually it was in good shape, but it wasn't cool looking ya know. That was the time of street rods and hot rods, and here we are driving around in a 4 door Plymouth Granny car.

I remember one time, it was a Sunday afternoon, and we were just hanging out in

Gucci's farm Pumpkin field, bored out of our minds and getting tired of hangin' out smashing pumpkins, so we decided that myself, Fred, Flaps and this guy Sal Amaturo would take a drive down to Atlantic City (which was about 2 hours away). You have to remember this was many, many years before Atlantic City, became the gambling hot spot it is at the time of writing this book. Back then you also have to know, that gasoline was like 24 cents a gallon, so you could get a full tank of gas for about 3 or 4 dollars, and with that much gas in the car the whole world was waiting for us to explore it.

Anyway, on the boardwalk, there was a place called Minskie's Burlesque, we never actually went in there, however we stopped at a place that was right outside, in front of the place, that sold Hot Dogs for 10 cents a piece. So of course at that price, you know we ate a shit load of hot dogs, and before you know it, we didn't have enough money to get home. So now, Sal came up with the bright idea that we crawl under the boardwalk and look for change people dropped between the boards on the boardwalk that fell underneath. Well to make a long story short there was nothing "Under The

Boardwalk" but sand and garbage. So here we all are crawling around in the sand under that damn boardwalk, like a bunch of damn sand crabs and the next thing I know, Sal is scurrying down underneath the boardwalk, about 15 feet ahead of us like his pants were on fire, and I look down at Sal, and there he was looking up between the cracks of the boards looking up at the woman's dresses and screaming "Hey look at this one, shes got no underwear on". I really guess you had to be there to appreciate just how sick that shit was back then, and what it looked like. (Oh, did we all crawl down to where Sal was and have a look?), Now really what do you think? Of course we did! The only problem was when we did, after getting beach sand all over us, in our hair and down our pants, The woman was like 60 years old, and ugly as sin. So after I smacked the hell out of Sal, we did managed to meet 3 teen age girls that night, on the boardwalk, and they lent us 4 dollars, which was just about enough to get us home.

Another story, or actually another event, (they all had a way of turning into major events), that took place was, I guess it was about 2 o'clock in the morning and we were just hangin' out drinking MD20/20, (you could buy that stuff for $1.00 a bottle, we call it Mad Dog 20/20, which was actually rot gut), and when we were really smashed, I mean really fucked up, we all decided after getting our ass's as drunk as we could, that we were going to become Olympic ski champions, so we decided at 2 AM to drive from New Jersey to the Catskill Mountains in New York, to a ski lodge called Hunter Mountain in the Catskills in New York State. So it was myself, Fred in the front and Flaps and a guy called Carmine, who just happen to weigh 540 pounds at age 18 we called him The Coug or Bud-doe for short.

Okay so it's bad enough with 4 of use sitting in this Plymouth Cranbrook, but on top of that we had bought a toboggan sled, that was 6 feet long at a place called, "J.M. Fields Department store", on Route 35 in Hazlet. We had it inside the car with the front of the sled sitting on the dashboard of the car, stretching on top of the front seats, to the back deck behind the back seats, so there was one of each of us on each side of the toboggan.

Anyway where heading up to Hunter Mountain and it's snowing like hell and we see a soldier hitchhiking on the side of the road, in the snow storm, and Fred said to me pick him up man, so I did, and this guy gets in the car with a big ass duffel bag. He had no idea until he got in, that fat ass Carmine was sitting in the backseat taking up 3/4's of the seat, and Flaps was next to him, which left this soldier guy about 8 inches to fit himself, and that big ass duffel bag he had, in the back seat.

So anyway, he gets into the car and naturally again, I told you we were all drunk, and we ask him where he needed to go, and he said he's going to visit his mother. Well about halfway through the trip, Fred turned around in his drunken stuber and says while drooling on himself, "Your mother got any food man", and as I looked back at the kid from the rear view mirror the poor kid looked scared to death, with a look on his face like, "what the hell did I get myself into".

We continued on with this bullshit going on in the car, for maybe about an hour and we stopped for gas, and when we got back into the car the kid was gone, he just disappeared into a raging snow blizzard. I guess by that time he had thought he had been picked up by a bunch of fuckin' psychos, which I think looking back at it today, he was pretty damn close to the truth.

So we headed out to Hunter Mountain SKI Bowl. Now remember here comes four drunk ass guys from New Jersey, and one of the guys was a 500+ pound wall of humanity, and we are all wearing leather motorcycle type jackets,

We arrive at Hunter Mountain and we pile out of the car, and here are all these people dressed in high fashion ski ware, and here comes the 4 of us carrying a toboggan sled. (Now that had to be some sight for sure).

Well we get to the mountain part and ski trails, and the guy tells us we can't bring that toboggan on the hill, so we go and actually rent skis and boots, and course we can't ski, we don't even have a clue how to ski, but we walk up to the chair lift carrying the skis and slipping all over the God damn place, from the ice on the ground. We got in the line, standing next to the chair holding our rented skis, and the guy that was running the chair lift snap the skis on our feet, and we just like took two steps, to the left and the chair came around and hit us in the ass, and we started going up the hill saying to each other, "this is pretty cool"

So we get to the top of the hill and to our surprise there is a sign saying "Please ski to the right when unloading" Ski to the right??? "You gotta be fuckin' kidding me we don't have a clue how to ski, we got problems walking for Christ sake".

Well we get to the top hill and the chair tosses us out, and to make a long story short again, all four of us fall flat on our asses in a pile, with Carmine on top crushing us. So now at the top of the mountain you got four drunken idiots in leather jackets in a pile of humanity blocking the way of other skiers trying to get off the chair lift,

We walked once again carrying our skis to the top of the hill, and I was totally amazed at how steep that son of a bitchin' hill actually was, I mean it was straight down, no slope to it, just a straight drop.

So were all standing at the top, and we had snapped into the skis trying to figure out how the hell we were going to do this shit, when a girl next to me said with a smile, "Just put your feet together and aim for the lodge", which was probably a good distance from the top of this mountain.

We had no choice but to follow her

instructions, I mean what the hell, it made sense to me. So we put our feet together and pushed off. Needless to say about 20 feet down the mountain we crashed into everybody that was in our path and we were rolling down this mountain. The next thing I know there's about four guys around us with red crosses on the back of the jackets, and they made us, (after yelling at us for a while), take off the skis and walk down the mountain, and we did that with pleasure! But trust me, walking down the bitch, Hell, that was more dangerous than skiing down it. But at lease we didn't kill anybody walking down it. Hell if we would have put them damn skis back on and try to ski down it, there would have been a mass homicide and we would have been searching for an alibi.

Well, I guess it's now time to get rid of this crazy shit that we were doing, and get to the real purpose of this book, and that purpose is my story in music. How did music come into my life, what happened, the untold stories, backroom deals, and the secrets the industry kept for the public. So stay tuned, HERE WE GO.

The Red Hawk Experience

The chapters in this second book are going to be laid out a little different then my first book. It's not gonna be in order of the years that the events actually happened, but will jump around and primarily focus on different events, that took place in my life at different times.

I remember thinking back to the late 70 early 80s, when I was booked in Hawaii for four weeks, at a place called Duke Kahanamoku's Hula Hut. It was located on the island of Oahu, in a place located in the international marketplace, which was actually right across the street from Waikiki Beach. It was really a unique club. It seated around 400 to 500 people BUT had no walls at all, it only had a palm tree type roof. Very Hawaiian. The tourist love the atmosphere.

We were in there to do two shows a night, 6 nights a week, with a guy that was very popular in that area known as Dick Jensen. He was kind of like a Hawaiian Tom Jones, with James Browns moves on stage, and I might add he was fantastic. He put on one hell show as I remembered. I was the headliner and we had to follow this guy, and it was not an easy job. There were two names you did not want to follow in Hawaii. One was Don Ho, and the other was Dick Jensen. Those two guys were like the second coming of Christ there.

Anyway while we were performing on our opening night, I had already done the first show, and I remember going outside in the market place area, to go to the little shops that were there selling Hawaiian souvenirs. While I was out there on a break, I noticed a guy over by a huge Banyan tree, that was located right in the middle of the walk way at the entrance of the market place, and all the tourist would be taking pictures in front of that damn tree.

But anyway, there was a guy standing

there in a black top hat and wearing a black cape. He stood out like a sore thumb, because in Hawaii everyone had on these very colorful flowered type Hawaiian shirts, and here is this guy wearing this outfit, plus he had about five or six orchid leis around his neck. And before you know it, there were tons of tourists rushing to get a picture with him standing in front of that fuckin' tree. So once the crowd died down, I walked over and complimented him on the hat he was wearing, because after all, anyone that knows me, knows I'm a hat guy. I mean I really love hats!

So I introduced myself to him, and told him I was performing at the club, and he told me his name was Ed, and I asked him did he always get this kind of attention when he showed up at the marketplace.

He answered, "yeah, the tourists always want to get a picture with a direct descendent of Duke Kahanamoku". I said, "cool, so you lived here right", and he responded, "yup I live in Honolulu".

Well we talked for about 45 minutes, and he told me that he also was a singer, and asked me if he could sit in for a song. I told him no, because we have a set show that we do, but I invited him backstage to see the show.

Then after our set, I went to breakfast with him and we talked for probably two hours. He was an interesting guy to say the least, and I must say that I liked hangin' with him. He was pretty cool.

We made plans to get together the next day, and he was gonna show me around the island, that's when I found out that he was in the Navy, stationed at Pearl Harbor. He actually admitted to me that day, that he was not Hawaiian but like to dress up like that to get the attention of the tourists, which I might add, he got a lot of when he was in that get up of his.

He told me he was from Arizona, and really his dream had always been to become an entertainer, which made sense to me, because of what he was doing in Hawaii, I mean dressing up like that and playing the part of Hawaiian royalty.

I have to say at this time that this guy was extremely intelligent, and had the ability to be very convincing, in the part that he was playing of his alter ego at that point in time. I mean even if he told me who he really was, I would still have gone on believing that he was the person he was portraying. He was that good at it.

Anyway I said to him, "come to a rehearsal and we will work out a song that you can sing in the show". He was ecstatic about it, and jumped at the chance to take a shot at it. I told him if it worked out, I would introduce him as the character he was portraying for the tourists, that would give him a little bit of an edge, and make it easier for him to get over, because in reality he looked Hawaiian.

The next day we had a band rehearsal and he showed up. I got the band to learn the Hawaiian love song, you know the one that Elvis did, and sure enough this guy could sing, I mean he was excellent, so we made plans to put him in the show that night. I will say that he went over like gangbusters, the tourist loved him. I remember he wore the same outfit, the black top hat and the Cape and he was covered in orchid leis. We billed him as Ed Kahanamoku , and before you know it they were lining up to get a picture with him and an autograph.

The way the show was set up, there was an actor from a television series that was popular back then called Hawaii Eye, and a guy that played the part of a taxicab driver name Pocci Ponce did a standup comedy act before Dick went on. He looked very

Hawaiian but was actually Japanese, but on the television show he played a Hawaiian taxicab driver. Well after about four nights of Ed doing is number, this Pocci guy became a little jealous of all the attention that Ed was getting, and came up to me one night backstage and said, "you know this guy ain't even Hawaiian", in a real sarcastic way, like he was pissed off about me letting Ed sing a song in MY FUCKIN SHOW!!, and I replied, "what the fuck are you complaining about, your Japanese for Christ sakes, and your prancing around like some kind of Oscar winning actor", Plus you little fuck YOU AIN'T FUNNY!!!. (as anyone who knew me back then I was not easy to get along with). The bottom line was it was entertainment man we were all playing a part, Dick wasn't Tom Jones or James Brown but he acted like Tom Jones on stage and Pocci Ponce was the farthest thing from a comedian that you could imagine, I mean the guy sucked!

The bottom line was all Ed really cared about doing that one damn song a night, and it was a double-edged sword and I loved it. I was the headliner there, and I was loving the break in the middle of the show Ed gave me. And his appearance allowed me to grab a quick drink and a cigarette backstage. Funny thing was the first couple of times he did his song, he just sang it and got off, then towards the end of our run there, he started to engage more with the crowd, and talk to them, and he was on the stage for like 15 to 20 mins. But they loved him, and I didn't give a shit, I was makin' the money sitting on my ass back stage.

Well we did our four weeks there, and it was time to move on. Funny thing happened, the last night we performed, Ed never showed up for some reason, and I was a little concerned that something had happened to him. I mean this guy love doing that song on that stage, and I could not imagine him missing a chance to perform it one last time. But needless to say he never show the last night and I never saw him again.

Now I want to roll the clock ahead 10 years. I had opened up a recording studio in the city of Hampton, Virginia, (and by the way had gotten married again, some people never learn) and I called it the Power Plant. I had stopped touring and performing on stage at that time, and really, to be honest with you, throughout my whole career, I never really wanted to be a performer. I always wanted to be a record producer in a recording studio, so once I quit touring, it gave me the opportunity to build myself a recording studio and produce all the records I wanted. And if you read my first book, you would know that I was doing a lot of producing on the side, in other studios while I was touring and performing.

So anyway getting back to the Power Plant. I had to go to the city of Norfolk one day, to do some business, and pick up some recording tape. While I was there I stopped and grabbed lunch at a place in Virginia Beach. And while I'm eating and talking to one of my partners, I see this guy sitting a couple of tables away from me and I said to myself, "God damn that guy looks like Ed from Hawaii, but this time he had long black hair and was not wearing the top hat in the Cape.

I got up and walked over to him, and I see him staring at me as I'm walking over, and before "I could say are you Ed"? He gets up from the table with a big smile and walked over to me and said Doc!, "what the hell are you doing in Virginia Beach", I said "never mind me what the hell are you doing here"? He said I live in Virginia now, I got out of the

Navy and I was here at the base when they discharged me, so I stayed. He said, "so are you performing here in town "?, I said "nah, I quit that shit five years ago and opened up a recording studio, on the other side of the water in Hampton.

I remember that conversation like it was yesterday, he had a big smile on his face and said, "so now you can finally make me a star". And I said, "Ed you are already a god damn star". We both laughed and I said, "listen stop by the Power Plant, we'll do lunch and talk about old times on the island "

I gave him the address of the studio, and he said he was going to stop by in the next couple of days. I had no idea at that time that I, would become a part of and influenced by a character that was already created, by Ed named Red Hawk, and it would lead me on a tremendous journey of emotion, friendship, hardship and success. But that's exactly what was about to happen.

Well, needless to say Ed did showed up at the studio like three days later. Only this time he had a totally different look. He was wearing a buckskin jacket with fringe, and loaded with Native American bead work. I mean the jacket was unbelievable, and to boot he had on a Native American head band, I mean the man looked like Geronimo.

So he comes in and I gave him a quick tour of the studio and then I just had to ask him, "so what the hell is with the outfit". He proceeds to inform me that he had legally changed his name to Red Hawk, and was pursuing a new career as a Native American storyteller. I mean he now had the look for sure, and one thing about Ed, he was far from stupid, he was a very intelligent man and he did his homework. When he created an alter ego he studied all the facts that were pertinent to that character, which made the character convincing enough to pull the whole thing off.

After he explained to me how he was going to go about this new career, I have to admit it kinda all made sense and during that time in America, interest in the Native American arts were at its highest point ever with white America.

But then he changed direction with me, and asked if I would be interested in recording him singing a few Native American tributes songs. I can remember saying why just sing the songs, why don't you record the story also that you been studying, and he agreed to try it. He had a beautiful speaking voice, but I wanted to get a particular sound of his voice, sort of like a James Earl Jones type voice, that would have a very commanding sound to it.

So, I started searching for a special microphone, that would give him that ambiance, and I found one that worked perfectly. It was a vintage Numan Tube Mic, and it gave them a huge deep sound.

But I said to him, let's do this a little different. You tell the story, and then I will add music behind it sort of like scoring a movie, and give it a unique sound to where the listener will feel like, they are there at the time of the story.

So we sat down, and started to go through literature of different Native American chiefs speeches, and different events, that took place in history that featured the Native American plight during the time, of the white man invading and stealing their land.

How ever the more we got into it, the more we found out that the history books in school, were telling the stories and facts all wrong. It did not happen at all the way the history books said it did, and this gave us a special twist that made the recordings different, than what was said to all of us white Americans, about what actually and how it actually happen back in those times.

While I was doing that research, Hawk was putting together, different actual Native American stories, that were handed down from generation to generation, through the different Native American tribes. One group of stories that we discovered, between the actual history books and the Native American legends, was about a group known as the Cheyenne dog soldiers.

This was an elite fighting force, much like today's Green Berets or special forces in our military. Upon further investigation, we came upon a document in the Library of Congress, that contradicted every history book ever written, about the fact, that the Indian chief Crazy Horse, was the actual leader of the band of warriors that defeated General Custard at the battle of Little Bighorn.

The truth of that battle was, it was not Crazy Horse, it was the Cheyenne dog soldiers that massacred General Custard at the little Bighorn, Crazy Horse was fighting general Reno in another location and then joined the Cheyenne dog soldiers at the end of the battle with General Custard.

So it was at that time, finding this information out, that myself and Ed figured, if they got that wrong, they got a bunch of other stuff wrong, and it was at that time we both knew we were on the something. And to top it all off we had the character in Red Hawk to pull it off on a major level.

No one has ever done a spoken word album before, with a full orchestra accompaniment with sound effects to make the piece even more realistic. Sure it was gonna be a lot of work, but artistically it was going to be phenomenal and a one-of-a-kind.

So after we had gathered all the material we needed, we began work on this series of albums, focusing on Native American history the way it really happened. The project would contain five or six albums. One being the history of the Cheyenne Dog Soldiers, another one the history and stories of the Buffalo, and one title the history and stories of the Crow, we also did one called the history and stories of the Wolf and finally one called These Were Their Words, and that final album contained the famous speeches given by different Indian Chiefs through out history.

All of the stories and the CD's were

focusing on Native American legends, and true stories of events that took place during that early era. And the bottom line was Red Hawk already had mastered the look, and had the talent and the ability, to deliver all the stories with a convincing voice, added to a convincing appearance. Looking at it as a record producer this was a slam dunk. I had the vehicle in Red Hawk that could deliver it, and we had the facts that would make the history books look like comic books, when compared to the actual facts of what took place.

I was under the impression that myself and Red Hawk were on the same page, when it came to his creation of his alter ego, full well knowing to the both of us, that he would be just like an actor playing the part of the Native American storyteller. But looking back at it now and coupled with his real life Mexican heritage, and really the truth be known in my opinion, Mexicans are basically Native American because they were there. The Incas and the Aztec Indians, were here in North America Way before the white man came, so in my opinion that's as native American as you can get.

The bottom line and major problem, if

there was going to be any was Red Hawk getting over trying to be Native American. But once again he was Mexican and that is as Native American you can get.

As we got into the projects and we started to release some of the records to the public, it was apparent to both of us, that we had a winner on these projects. The public response was fantastic, we started to sell huge amounts of CD's, as a matter of fact, the University of Texas actually purchase a bunch of the Cheyenne Dog Soldiers CD's, and had a course on it based on the facts that were on our CD. So without a doubt, me in Red Hawk were on to something good, and we were on our way with it. But it slowly became apparent to me, that Red Hawk was slowly becoming the alter ego that he had created, and I knew that if he took it too far it could be dangerous, to both himself and to the projects future.

I want to make myself perfectly clear, at this point, in no way where we trying to deceive the public. We were only messengers of the truth, and presenting it in a theatrical way, that was both entertaining and informative, and most of all setting the records straight for the first time in history. All the projects became a sort of what history forgot, and we felt that we were going to bring it to light and correct the mistakes.

Okay now the race is on. Red Hawk going full steam ahead, and it seems like there is no stopping the success train. Not only is he selling a lot of CD's, he is now also doing a lot of speaking engagements, and demanding a pretty decent price for his appearances. However now it became clear to me that Red Hawk, was starting to believe his own press, and he was slowly transforming into the character he had created. Speaking engagements were becoming a weekly thing with him, being a keynote speaker at many events made it even better.

But as always my main concern was the recording aspect of his whole career, and making sure that all the stories retold on the CD's were historically correct. It was Red Hawks job to be the vehicle, in order to deliver the words and the concept of what we were doing. And the basic concept was, stating the facts of the real Native American history, that history that had been forgotten or hidden for many years and what had been taught mistakenly or to put it bluntly, Lied About!!. And in many cases delivering that message, which was contrary to the way that the mass population had known it to be for many years, was far from an easy task. But Red Hawk, was brilliant at being able to deliver the message, not only in a factual way, but to make it entertaining, which made the truth easier to swallow.

I remember one day he came to me, to tell me he was changing his name again, to Chief Red Hawk. He told me that he had been asked to joined a Native American organization based in Georgia, and they were going to make him a chief. I can remember asking him, what the fuck kind of organization can make you a Cherokee Indian chief, your a God Damn Mexican? he said he joined, and they told him he was going to be name a chief of a certain band with that organization.

I can clearly remember that day, I told him, Hawk you are taking this shit too far. You need to concentrate on being a performer portraying a character, and using that character to deliver your message. This is pure entertainment my friend, and you trying to get yourself in a history book as being some sort of native American legend.

His response to me was "this all adds to the character and gives it credibility, so I am going for it". I said "okay but I'm going down on record to say this is taking it over the top and it could come back to bite us in the ass".

His CDs were selling like hot cakes, they were all over the Internet and people were eating them up. Then out of nowhere we get a letter from the Native American Music Awards stating that one of our releases Chief Seattle Speaks is nominated for an award in the best historical recording category. Now all hell breaks loose with Red Hawk. He is on cloud nine and by this time he is becoming a legend in his own mind and started being difficult to advise and control. I really think that he was finally achieving the notoriety and fame he had always dreamed of his whole life. He considered himself to now be at the top of his game, however in reality it really wasn't him, it was the character Red Hawk that the public was embracing. I could see that clearly, but he was unable to grasp the reality at that point of the journey, and he was having a problem telling the difference between his fantasy and reality.

Okay now shit is really starting to get crazy. Before you know it Red Hawk had every phoney Tom, Dick and Harry hanging on to him like he was second coming of Christ, and no matter who they were all of a sudden they became native Americans. I mean we had Black Hawks, Purple Hawks, Green Hawk's you name it, and they were coming out of the wood work. The more notoriety he got, the more the leeches would be hanging on him. One guy actually dye his hair black and used so much man tan on his face to look Native American that he looked orange. To top it all off they all are now claiming to be his brother. The only real Indian out of the whole bunch was guy named Swamp Rat. He was the real deal, but Hawk was so good at playing that character he even convinced Swamp Rat he was a real native American. This shit was getting so out of hand that it was like a living cartoon, but it was about to get a lot worst.

Now comes the good part or bad part depending on how you or whoever looked at it. They are having the native American music awards in Niagara Falls, New York and Hawk talks me into going to it. I can remember telling him, "you're really pushing your luck with this bullshit", but, he wanted to go bad, Old Hawk had one hell of an ego. So myself, Red Hawk and a guy named Arthur Palazzo, that I listed on Red Hawks album as a co-producer, (even though he really did not do anything on the album that was nominated for an award".

The event was broadcast live on the Internet and I really had my doubts if we were going to win that thing. I mean really the place was packed with real Indians and here we are, two white guys and a Mexican sitting there nominated for a native American music award. OK, so here's the crazy shit, they announced the winner of the Nammy, in the category best historical recording. Well sure enough, Red Hawk wins the God damn thing! Now remember this is a native American music award show, and a fuckin' Mexican pretending to be an Indian, has just won the award, but I have to say, that proves how great his recordings were, and how convincing he was portraying the character he had invented.

So the long and short of it was, that Hawk had won the award and trust me that was a really big deal. But the big picture was starting to unfold. When you get that much attention and you get that much notoriety it also sparks people that will dig deeper into the phenomena of Red Hawk and that would get us in the middle of a questioning, jealous,

Internet landslide.

It was then that the Internet started to buzz, with people questioning the heritage of this man called Red Hawk. It was then, that I stepped up and told him, you need to come out and get off of that Chief Red Hawks shit, and slowly convert into who you really are, which was an actor portraying a part. It was then I told him, that your fans would accept that because in reality you were doing more good for native American people then the native American people were doing for themselves. Once again he would not listen, he was to deep into that character he had created, in his mind I think he really believe that he was Chief Red Hawk.

I want to make one thing perfectly clear here, that this man now known as Red Hawk to the public was an extremely kind man, he was an intelligent man and I had the utmost respect for him as a human being. But make no mistake about it, this guy could sell air conditioners to the Eskimos in the dead of winter. He, without a doubt was the greatest salesman I had ever met in my entire career. But in reality folks, isn't that what you're supposed to do when you're playing a part. My opinion for whatever that's worth, he will always deserve the recognition of being a great entertainer from his start in Hawaii to where ever this new path would lead him.

At this point his career was full blast, he had high paying speaking appearances, his record sales were through the roof and a few videos that we had posted on a popular website called You Tube, had gathered over a quarter of a million views.

I was constantly telling him to back off on the Native American heritage, and just when I thought I would make some head way with him on it, he would come up with a new twist to the whole story.

Example? He walked into my recording studio one day and announced to me that he was given an honorary Kentucky Colonel award, and he was now a full fledged Kentucky Colonel. But in a way it did not surprise me at all. You see that's who Ed was. I think deep down inside he never really liked who he really was and by creating the different characters he was able to create someone really special, and in the end he was finally able to feel good about who he really was.

This chapter on Red Hawk was extremely good for him, and he touched a lot of peoples hearts with knowledge and compassion for his art form. He brought a lot of joy to people who needed that badly, he brought a lot of truth to the history, and the plight of the Native American people of this country. He was a genius at what he did. But in the end the fans and the people that he adored and were enlightened with his knowledge, and performance skills would turn on him, and turn out to be his death song.

The negative articles that were printed on the Internet blasting him for not being of Native American heritage, and the cruelty that was aimed at him on a personal level, were far from the accolades that he so rightfully deserved and earned for the work that he did, using his skill as a great communicator to tell the truth about history as only he could have brought it to the public's eye.

The outside pressure of people attacking him became so great that he sadly took his own life. But he left us a countless library of recordings and videos, that will go down in history as some of the greatest works of art ever accomplished by any human being in that field.

I personally miss you Red Hawk, and I thank you for allowing me the honor to participate in your extraordinary journey, through that part of your life. Rest in peace my friend your words will live on.

RED HAWK ACCEPTING THE "NAMMY" AWARD FOR BEST HISTORICAL RECORDING

DOC HOLIDAY AND RED HAWK WITH THE "NAMMY AWARD"

DOC HOLIDAY, BILL REID AND RED HAWK TALK IT OVER BEFORE THE DOORS OPEN UP AT RED HAWKS SOLD OUT SHOW "THE GATHERING OF THE FOUR WINDS"

DOC HOLIDAYS THE POWER PLANT STUDIOS, HAMPTON, VIRGINIA

A Road Trip, That Lasted 20 Plus Years

OK, this may sound like a strange title, but that's exactly what it was. We left to do a two week performance at a small town in South Carolina and that would be the start of the 20 plus year tour playing music.

In this chapter I am going to hit on some of the towns, clubs and countries that I performed at during my 20 plus years as a touring musician. Some of the names and places may sound familiar to you, and then again some of them may not. On the road touring was a major part of my career, although it may not have felt that way when I was doing it back then, however it was really a necessary evil that allowed me to hone my skills, and increase my knowledge as a musician and performer, both on stage and off stage. Because in reality, when you are an entertainer you are always on stage 24/7!

I'm going to jump around a lot in this chapter, and just hit on some of the more memorable things that happen on the road. I didn't know it then, but as I look back at it now, I guess this was paying my dues, along with a miss spent youth.

There were many musicians that came in and out of my life in the different bands I had, and each of them had their own unique personality, which made them memorable throughout all my touring years. From Chickie and the boys in Jersey, all the way up to Ray Harris, Frank Rosa and the rest of the guys from Florida. There were many, many players that passed through, and I'm sure I'm not going to be able to remember all of them, but I will try my best to name some of the ones that stick out in my mind as I'm writing this book. And before I go any further I also want to acknowledge the agents and managers that kept me going, because without them, the world would have never known or heard of an entertainer named Doc Holiday.

I'm going to start off with a club named the Thunderbird lounge and it was located in Florence, South Carolina. We work this club for two weeks, six nights a week. And I have to say, that this place was jammed every night, and these people knew how to party. Not a single night went by in that place, that there would not be at least 5 to 6 different sweet southern groupies, that would be there for the taking, and that made it a lot easier to go to work.

However that being said, there also were always these two little old ladies that I have to mention, who came in every night and sat there from our first song to our very last, right in front of the stage. They were sweethearts, and as it would turn out, any time we played North Carolina, South Carolina or Georgia they would show up. They became my biggest fans. I remember their names, one was Annie B any other was named Irene, and they would dance all night long non stop. They were probably both at least 60 plus years of age back then and me and the band love them. They would dress up every night like they were going to some Royal ball, and I loved it because they were living life to its fullest. Believe it or not these old girls, because of their friendship with myself and the band actually made some of the groupies in the audience jealous, because all my guys in the band, and myself paid a lot of attention to them. Like I said they were sweethearts and we loved them. They are both gone now, as of the writing of this book, but they will never be forgotten by me.

One of the most memorable things that happened at the Thunderbird, was, I was sitting around outside my room, and it was about two in the morning, and my drummer Kenny at the time came up and said, "Doc the housekeeping room is open", you know the room where the maids kept all the towels and sheets, and everything else needed to keep the motel clean. He said "Do you need any towels"

Well to make a long story short, one of our agents had his offices in a town called Fayetteville, North Carolina. It was probably about a 45 minute drive from where we were, at the Thunderbird. And in the front of his office building, there was a huge fountain, I mean this thing was really big, and it probably shot water 30 feet in the air. Just then my drummer informed me that there was a 50 gallon drum of laundry detergent in that housekeeping room. So we get the bright idea to take this 50 gallon drum of pure soap, and we put it in one of our vans and drive up to Fayetteville, North Carolina to dump the detergent into that fountain, in front of our agents office building, we figured it would make it look sudsy and would be a cool thing to do.

Well we get there and it's like 3:30 in the morning and there wasn't a soul in sight, I mean the streets were like a ghost town. So we pulled the van up to the side of the fountain right on the sidewalk and started to dump the detergent into the fountain, and just then the sky and everything around us was full of bubbles floating in the air. I mean to tell you it was a sight to see. The bubbles were shooting 30 to 40 feet in the air and they were all over the place. So we quickly close the side door in the van and got the hell out of there before the cops came. Oh, by the way the empty drum was still in the van, We got rid of that at a place called South Of The Border on Hwy 95 in South Carolina, We just left it in the parking lot there.

The next day believe it or not, it made the front page of the paper in Fayetteville and it probably took them two or three weeks to clean that mess up. Those bubbles were all over that town.

You can imagine, here we are, six grown men who probably missed blowing bubbles in their childhood, have now made up for it in the biggest way possible. And I must admit, that alcohol was not a factor, (yeah right, we were drunk on our ass's, smile). Needless to say we were a big hit in that club the Thunderbird, and would end up playing it three times a year or the next 10 years. But then the club was sold to a new owner and they changed the format of the entertainment, and being a road band we would hit that endless black ribbon call the highway once again, never to return to Florence, South Carolina again.

The next town we always hit was Hampton, Virginia at a place called Hornes. The results of our performances there were the same, we became local stars and packed the place every night. The owner of the club was named Bill Gust and we soon became the only touring band that would pack that club every night of the week. Bill had a house agent by the name of Ginny Earls. She was a great looking woman, tall with blonde hair and a great body, but she also knew her stuff when it came to booking entertainment.

After working that club four and five times a year we got to know most of the crowd that came in there on a personal basis. And when we were scheduled to perform there, all they had to do was put my name on the Billboard outside, and there would be lines of people standing outside lined up to get in.

After our first performance there, they started doing, for the first time in the history of the club, placing a five dollar cover charge on the door in order to get in, because of the crowds we were drawing. And it was plain to see at that time, that not only was Ginny Earls the booking agent for that club but she was also the manager and responsible for the club doing as well as it did. Some of you who read the first book knew that I was not the easiest person in the world to work with. I would be throwing fits demanding certain perks that I felt I deserved. So needless to say, me and Ginny did not get along all the time. However because we were packing the place every night of the week, Ginny would bend more for me than any other touring band that perform there.

Well one particular night we were scheduled to open for a name act (I can't say his name right now, he's still alive and performing and very well known) but he had just won the Academy award for song he did in a movie that was a huge box office hit. Needless to say we were sold out that night at the ticket price of $30 apiece to get in, which back then in the 70's was a lot of money.

While at that time it was common knowledge that this particular star had gone through some serious Cocain drug problems. But it was reputed that he was completely clean and had found Jesus.

Well I picked him and his manager up at the airport, and his manager had gotten wind of my reputation with the use of drugs at that time, and quickly walked up to me and said "don't offer him any drugs, he's clean now", and sure enough he came off the plane with the Bible in his hand. So naturally I refrained from bringing up the subject of any drugs. Then I remember, that he got me on the side away from his manager at the airport and said "Doc you got any coke", and I said "man I heard you were clean now". Well to my surprise he opened up the Bible, and the center of the Bible pages were cut out, and in the cut out space was a the bag of coke that was almost empty. He had a big smile on his face, but I kept my mouth shut about it, and of course I had to do a little bit of his coke to get me over, and we proceeded to head toward the club for an afternoon sound check.

Everything went smooth during the sound check and we got ready for a sold-out performance that night. The club was a 1000 seat club and it was packed wall-to-wall with people with a solid $30 cover charge to see me and him perform.

So that night, I went on and started my part of the show, and at the end of my set, we were supposed to immediately play the instrumental part of his current hit song to bring him on for his set. And after playing the intro for about 40 seconds, I got ready to introduce him, and I looked over to my right to see if he was coming on stage or at lease standing in the wings, and I saw his manager giving me a hand signal to stall the show, and keep playing the intro. It seems he needed the start of the show to be stretched to give him more time.

Well, we played the intro probably for at lease two or three minutes and by this time we are starting to push our luck with the audience. I mean really they pay $30 to see this guy and here we were playing the intro to his hit for close to five minutes. I kept the band playing and I walked off to the right side of the stage to his manager and said, "what the fuck is going on", he said to me "we had a slight problem, but were getting him ready now" then in the next 40 seconds or so, he finally walked up to me and said "I'm ready Doctor". Oh yea he was ready all right. He looked like he was stoned out of his fuckin' mind, but he hit that stage and I'll tell you one thing, once that spotlight hit his face, he was flawless, the man was brilliant and put on one hell of a show. No one in the audience that night ever knew what had transpired backstage and how close that show came to being canceled.

Okay, then came a club in Savannah, Georgia. In a mall located right outside the city, however our rooms were located at the Holiday Inn downtown. It just happened to be that we were also playing in a Holiday Inn, however it was on the outskirts of the main town.

Now I'm gonna let you in on a little secret, when we were on the road, we used to have a little game we played you know, just between the band members. It was sort of a contest we did every week. It was real simple. Where ever we were playing, we would tell a groupie we hooked up with, that it was our birthday that week, and at the end of the week, who ever got the best birthday present won the contest.

All the performances were booked for like $3,250.00 per week or even higher but there was always $50 or $75 extra on each paycheck left over after we paid everyone. So whoever got the best birthday present would get the extra money at the end of the week, as the prize that week. I personally never participated in the contest. Yup, I know it sounds cruel but that's what they wound up doing. I guess that little game kept them from going crazy on the road. And looking back at it, I guess the band members were sort of like, down town Hookers for a better term (smile)

Well at this particular club in Savannah, everyone in the band got lucky and hooked up with a girl that week. One afternoon I was standing in the motel parking lot with my bass player Myron Hale, and he was showing me a gold chain that he had gotten from a town girl that week as his "Birthday" present. And I remember saying "Myron you're going to win the contest this week". Just then I looked up on the second floor of the motel and walking to their room was Blake Marean, who was one of our roadies and Larry Pasmore who was the drummer in the band at the time.

They were walking down the motel walkway with two girls following them (I might add TWO VERY LARGE GIRLS), and they looked down at me and Myron and they were doing some sort of a happy dance, yelling "We scored, We scored", like they had just won the fuckin' lottery. And in their hand was a Burger King bag, and the two of them were smiling like Cheshire cats from an Alice In Wonderland movie. Wow, now that was their big score, two whoppers and a French fry. Needless to say they did not win the contest that week. To be honest with you, those two characters never won the contest any week.

Okay then came a club in Boston, Massachusetts. It was called the Triple O's, and this incident took place while I was being managed by Whitey Bulger, (actually I believed that Whitey might have owned that club). Well I guess you guessed it by now this was a time when organized crime, and the music business connection reared its ugly head again. It was a pretty cool club, and it was a great place to perform, plus the fact it was jammed packed every night.

We were working there with a DJ name Jimmy Jay. Every single night I ever worked there, I never had a reason to go downstairs in the basement of the club. I was curious because I would often see people going down there, but I never went down. Well one night Jimmy Jay, for some strange reason, unbeknownst to me, decided to go down to the basement to have a look around. Well sure enough when he got down there, a few of the so-called wise guys that were in the club that night, asked me where Jimmy was? I said "he's down in the basement ". They immediately grabbed my arm and told me to follow them down the stairs, and sure enough there was Jimmy standing there staring at a big blue tarp that was spread out in the middle of the floor with the chair in the center of it.

I remember Jimmy asking one of the guys there with me, "what's that chair there for"? and I think it was a guy that was with me who was known locally as the rifleman responded to Jimmy "you better fuckin' hope your never sitting in that fucking chair, now get the fuck outta here and never come back down here again"! Well that was enough for me, I mean I was just there to play music, I did not want any part of that shit. But that stupid ass Jimmy keeps asking them God Damn questions about the chair, and I finally said "would you please shut the fuck up already".

Well we finished up the show that night and a couple of the regulars asked me if I wanted to grab some Chinese food. Well hell, it was 2 o'clock in the morning and these were the same guys who went downstairs with us, so I had to ask "where the hell are you gonna get Chinese food at two in the morning "?. One of the guys said "don't worry about it there's a place in the combat zone that will open up when we get there". Okay right about now I'm starting to shit in my pants, and that God Damn Jimmy who has started all this shit to begin with, by going down stairs, had already taken off and gone home.

Just then this guy name Sam who claim to be a booking agent, but in reality owned a strip club in an area of Boston call the combat zone, said to me "don't worry about it man, it's cool". So they wanted to drive me there but I said no, and reluctantly said I will follow you in my car.

So I jumped in my car and started following them to the combat zone, sure enough it was a Chinese restaurant open and serving food.

We all walked in together, and I'm telling you right now, they treated these guys like royalty. We sat down in a private room in the back and they covered the table with food. Just then a couple of strippers walked in that were working for Sam in his club, that was located right across the street from the restaurant we were in.

I remember one girl in particular was a knockout. She was a tall blonde probably close to 6 feet tall. I said to Sam, "Sam that broad is a fuckin' knockout"! Sam turned to me and said, "calm down Doc, that broad is a fuckin' **guy**". I said "Whoa, I ain't going there my man", Needless to say from that point on, I just shut my mouth and just ate Chinese food. And that was a night to forget in Boston.

OK, I want you to try and imagine this. We are touring in the United States, there is a gas crisis going on, you cannot buy gasoline on a Sunday, and you can only buy gas on certain days if your license plate ends in an odd or even number. I might add also that it is that dead of winter, when most normal people including touring bands would start to head south where the weather was good and it was warm.

Not us, this band of geniuses head north, yeah you heard me right like a bunch of fuckin' idiots, we pack up and head to Canada.

Now mind you it's a Sunday and you can't buy gasoline on a Sunday, so we fill up the gas tanks on the bus and equipment vans on Saturday and head for the Canadian border. Well we make it to a border crossing on the Maine and Canadian border in a town called Calais, Maine. The bus and all the vans were totally running on empty, and it's snowin' like a mother fucker.

We hit that border and the first words out of my mouth to the border guards was, "you guys got any gas over here, because we are almost bone dry in the fuel department". The border crossing guard looked at me and said "we got all the gas you need as soon as you cross this line". And that my friends was a fact! There were gas stations all over the place with all the fuel we needed. And I remember turning to one of my band mates, and saying "what the fuck, there ain't no gas in the United States, and 100 feet away in Canada they got gas all over the God damn place". That just goes to show you how the gasoline companies and government were screwing the people in the United States.

Well anyway we got the fuel we needed, and started heading to a place called Port Hawksberry, Nova Scotia, and the club was the Buccaneer Lounge. I have to tell you it was so god damn cold you could not stay outside of the bus more than five minutes because of the fear of frostbite. What a fucking brilliant idea this was, going north in the winter.

Anyway we finally made it to the club. And it was a pretty cool place, it sat like maybe 400 or 500 people, it was a pretty big club. We went into the club and spoke to the bartender to find out where the rooms were we were staying at. She told me that there was a band house, because there were no motels in that town. I hated fucking band houses, but we had no choice in the matter, that's all there was, so we headed over to the band house.

We got some well deserved sleep that

night, and woke up in the morning and headed down to the club to set up the equipment. When we got there I met the manager of the club. He was a fairly big guy, around 30 years old, and he was really glad to see us. He was a great guy, and I sat and talked to him for like an hour while the roadies were setting up the equipment.

I came to find out that he was a boxing fanatic, and was a huge fan of Mohammed Ali. He had also heard from the agent, Skip York, that booked us in there, that I knew Mohammed Ali personally, so he could not stop asking me questions about Ali.

He also knew that at one time, I myself had boxed in the Golden gloves, I will tell you now, that was many years ago.

Well, after we stopped talking, he invited me over to his house to meet his wife. I walked into his house, and I was blown away, I mean this guy had statues, dolls, posters and pictures of Mohammed Ali all over his house. It was kinda like his own personal shrine to Ali.

It was then he informed me, that he had a boxing ring set up in his backyard, and asked me if I would spar a few rounds with him. I thought about it for a minute, and there was a bunch of his neighbors at his house to meet me, and I said yea, what the hell.

We go to the backyard and remember it's ice cold out there, but what the heck it was only going to be sparring for one round. Okay, so we put on the gloves, and I will tell you this boxing ring was four stupid ass poles in the ground with rope tied to each one to form a ring.

Okay so there's like 15 people watching including his wife, and we start to box. Now remember we were just supposed to be sparring, but this guy came out with fire in his eyes like he was in a championship match in Las Vegas.

The next thing I know he's swinging like a madman, and missing every single punch he threw, and his wife is screaming at me, "knock him out Doc, knock him out". So okay, he came pouring in like a mad bull, and I hit him with a shot right on his jaw that should have broke his neck, but he just shook his head and kept coming, like it didn't even get his attention. Right now I'm in a world of trouble, this guy could fuckin' kill me right here in the middle of nowhere, so I just kept moving around and he kept swinging like a wild man and missing every punch he threw. He never laid a glove on me the whole round,,,Thank God For That!

It was only later that night, that I found out his claim to fame in that area was, that he could break a coke bottle on his head. You heard me right this guy would take a coke bottle, and hit himself on his head until the bottle broke.

We played that club for a week, and every night after my show he would ask me to spar with him again. By the way, I never did, I value my life too much to do that shit again.

Okay, with Nova Scotia a distant memory, you would figure by now we would have gained a bit of intelligence and head south to the warmer weather. WRONG!!!! Instead we accept a booking in Corner Brook, Newfoundland. That's right below the fuckin' north pole, and it just happened to be the place where the Titanic hit the iceberg and sank.

Now here is the kicker of the whole deal. In order to get to Newfoundland you have to take a ferry boat across the North Atlantic Ocean, and it was a 12 hour trip. This was not a normal ferryboat, it was huge, I mean they actually put trains on this thing. But what the hell, one thing you can say we as a band would never be accused of, was making an intelligent move.

Okay we load up on the boat, pull on the bus and the equipment vans, and head off to Newfoundland. Now this ferryboat had probably seven different decks. Four levels for the cars, trains, trucks and buses, and then two levels containing a lounge, restaurant and a bar, and then there was the third level that was an observation deck.

The boat got underway, and we started heading toward Newfoundland. It was about two hours after leaving Sidney, Nova Scotia, that we started to hear scraping on the side of the boat. We ran to the windows, and looked out to see nothing but ice surrounding the boat, and we were crashing into the ice in order to move forward.

Just then the boat had leaned over to the side and was leaning at a 45° angle and was totally stopped. Yup, we were stuck in the ice. It was just then that we heard over the loudspeakers in the lounge area, that the boat was stuck in the ice, and they had called for an icebreaker to free a path to get us out.

Well it took the icebreaker probably four hours to reach our location, and I must admit during that time the thought of, "what the fuck was I thinking" entered my mind at least a dozen times. Well, you think we made a great decision going north, here comes another brilliant decision. I decide along with the band to go up to the observation deck to see if we can spot the icebreaker coming. We get up on the deck and the wind is blowing like 70 miles an hour, it's cold as shit, and here are 8 fucking idiots standing on this deck freezing our asses off. Now mind you, we are the only ones up there, because no one else on the boat was stupid enough to go up on that deck.

Now rather than go back down to the lounge area, the band of idiots, decide that we were going to stay up on the deck, and build a windbreaker out of a bunch of life preservers and cushions that we had found, tucked in the benches that were up there.

Before I go any further I have to make one thing perfectly clear. Alcohol and drugs was now a huge factor.

So anyway we start building the windbreaker, and we were going to hide behind the windbreaker, and block the wind, and wait for the icebreaker to come. After about 15 minutes of that bullshit, we decided, "fuck it" and we started to head back down to the bar deck. Now mind you the boat is still leaning at a 45° angle, then add in the fact that we were all drunk and stoned on our asses, and you can imagine what the hell that looked like.

The icebreaker finally arrived, and busted out a path, so the ferryboat could move forward. And by that time the boat had straightened up, however we were so fuckin blitz, that we were still standing at a 45° angle.

Well we finally landed in Newfoundland. It's funny the guys that work on the boat where from Newfoundland, and they called it the rock, and that's exactly what it was. One huge rock in the Atlantic Ocean. the Size of the state of Texas, dotted along the shoreline with multicolored little houses. Very little trees, but a whole lot of rock.

So now we start to drive our caravan up the coastline, and see very little of anything. I mean to tell you this place was really no mans land, but I will say this, it was a beautiful sight, rolling hills and mountains that touched the sky.

We finally reached Corner Book and located the club, called Harry's Lounge. It was located in a Kmart shopping center on the top of a huge hill. This place was one big ass club, it had to hold a few thousand people, and it made you wonder, what the hell is a club like this doing in the middle of nowhere, and more so, where the hell did the people come from, to fill this son of a bitch up? Oh yea, I forgot to tell you, to top it all off, we were lucky enough be right in the middle of one of the biggest snowstorms they had ever had. But the bottom line was we made it there, if any people came there that night, we were gonna rock the rock!

So we set up equipment and took a quick sound check and they directed us to a motel that was very close to the club. The motel was beautiful, it looked like a huge log cabin, and it was gorgeous inside. A big stone fireplace, raw beams, an extremely rustic looking. I loved this place, and I could have stayed there the next two years.

Well, we all checked into our rooms, got some sleep and some great food, not necessarily in that order, but we were finally relaxed.

We all put in a wake-up call for 7 o'clock that night, to give us a couple of hours to get ready, for the performance that night. When I woke up I looked out the window and it was unbelievable, you couldn't see anything, it was a pure white out, I'm talking a major blizzard. Well there was no way we were going to open that night, I mean you couldn't even see the club, let alone get to it. There was no way anyone could drive in that shit, so I called the club and said, " we are not gonna open tonight, right?", And the manager replied "hell yea, we are sold out".

And I informed him that we could not get our bus down the hill from the motel and up the hill to the club, and he said, I'll have somebody pick you guys up, just wait in the lobby and we will be there in the next 10 minutes.

So we were all dressed and ready to go, and we all go down to the lobby, and sure enough here come three haft tracks. Now if you don't know what that is, it's a little vehicle that holds two or three people, but it doesn't have any wheels, it has tracks like a tank, and they all got little snow plows on the front. Okay this is a new one for us. They told us we were going to make two or three trips to get us to the club. Course I went on the first trip to check it all out, and when I got up to the top of the hill where the club was, there had to be 1000 snowmobiles in that parking lot. That shit was crazy, nothing could stop these people from going out and raisin' hell.

So we went on that night and I'm telling you right now, we tore that place up. The only really funny thing about that place was, there were like eight women to every guy there. Who was complaining? Sure as hell none of the band or myself. I found out later after talking to one of the locals, most of the men left the island, because there was no work there, therefore 8 women to every male. Welcome to paradise! We wound up staying in Newfoundland for the next three months and performed in 10 different clubs there, traveling on the Trans Canada Highway, which was the only main road, that actually went from coast to coast on the island.

So we continued on playing every club in Newfoundland. Some of the clubs were big, and some of them not so big, like one in particular place call the Brittany Inn, in a town called Lewisport. The club seated about a hundred people at the most, but it was a really cool place, because the club was attached to the motel, and they never really got any big touring bands, because it was off the grid. Actually, the big deal in that town was, that they had just got a traffic light in the middle of the town. But the people were great, and we needed a break, so it was a welcome sight to say the least. Oh, one more thing, that was the first time we ever ate moose meat, and the last time.

Well, we had battled nature for three long months, and before you know it, we went from snowstorm to spring. I will tell you right now, that island was beautiful in the springtime.

You could ride down any road, and sooner or later, there would be a car on the side of the road selling cooked lobster out of their trunk, for one dollar each. That's right, you heard me right, cooked cold water lobster for a buck a piece. It sounds unbelievable but that was the truth, and besides the eight women to every guy, the lobster was the thing we would miss the most.

Okay so you figure we lasted through the winter, and now it was spring, and we had a huge following of fans there, so we would stick around for the spring and summer season. WRONG!

When all the other touring bands were heading north, we got a booking in Miami, Florida, at the Playboy club there. Even though we were actually booked on the island for seven more weeks, I made the decision, to work the Playboy club in Miami. I know another brilliant move. Let's pack up and go to a God damn oven, where the temperature were running in the high 90s.

I mean really, why stay in a place where our fans loved us, we were making money hand over fist, plus were eating lobster for a dollar apiece. Why the fuck would anyone want to leave this place, and to be honest with you, looking back at it, I still don't know why the hell we left. But leave we did. Yup booze and drugs played a part in that brilliant decision.

I can remember when we got back on the mainland of Nova Scotia, I was sitting in the back of the bus, looking out the window, and I saw a group of small islands in the bay of Fundy. I can remember going up front to our road manager, and saying "Greg, find out if I can buy one of those islands". I guess he just figured I was stoned, and never really got back to me on it.

It was funny though, because at the time, I had close to $200,000.00 in cash in the back of the bus, right next to me. And I did not know then but those little islands in the bay of Fundy, would play a major part in my life.

So we hit the Florida, Georgia line, And that bus and the equipment vans, had the pedal to the metal, we were bookin' it. We were cruising right along, and as usual I was laying down in the back of the bus in my little room there, and it was raining like hell, and that was good sleeping weather to me. So I started to doze off when I heard a huge bang, and the bus came to a screeching halt on the Florida Turnpike.

I thought shit, we hit something. I ran up to the front of the bus with everybody else, and Myron, my bass player, was driving the bus, and when I got up there, I found out that the windshield on the bus had blown in, and was wrapped around Myron from his head to his knees. It was still intact but it had broken into 1 million little pieces of glass that had molded to his face and chest in one big ass piece

I yelled, "Myron are you okay"? And he said "get this fuckin' glass off me". So we pulled the windshield off, still in one piece, and believe it or not he did not have a cut on him. For some reason, that damn thing just blew out. Like I said it was raining like hell and the wind was blowing like 20 miles an hour.

So here we are on the Florida Turnpike, with no windshield on the bus, the rain is pouring in, and the wind is blowing the rain all the way to the back of the bus, and we have to make Miami in the next seven hours. I said "we are fucked, there is no way were gonna fix this son of a bitch", and Myron looks up at me and said, "I can drive this bastard, I'll get us there". I said, "Myron, are you crazy? that wind is blowing 20 miles an hour out there, and if you're doing 60 that rain is gonna to hit you at like 80 miles an hour". But he said, "don't worry about it man, I'll just slow it down and I'll get our asses there. So off we went, poor Myron was getting beat to shit with wind and rain, but that crazy bastard got us there.

Well, we finally made it to Miami and the Playboy Club, and I will tell you right now, The rain had stopped and it was hotter than hell. I mean you just rolled down your window and you were sweating your ass off. But hey, we were in Miami, at the Playboy club surrounded by bunnies, it don't get any better than that. RIGHT?

Our rooms were in a motel called the Castaways, right on the beach in Miami beach. And this place was off the hook. I mean we had gone from mountains and waterfalls, to palm trees and bikinis, welcome to the Magic city.

So we open that night at the Playboy club, and it's jammed pack. Beautiful Playboy Bunnies all over the place, classy people, I mean this place was the real deal. I go up to do my show, and I have to say the band had them rockin' on their first set. Normally I would only go up once, or sometimes twice a night and do my show. The band always did the first set and the last set by themselves.

So my show goes over like gang busters, I won big time with this crowd. Right after I do my show, I went to the dressing room to grab a cig and a drink, and one of the bunnies came in and said the manager would like me to stop by his table before you leave. So right away, I'm thinking there's a problem, but I can't imagine what, because I just killed them out there.

So Blake Marean comes back to get me, and drive me back to the motel, and I told him, we have to stop my the managers table before we leave. So we stop at the managers table, and he is sitting there with like 3 bunnies, and he gets up and shakes my hand and said "Great Show Doc, Great Show" and he's got a big smile on his face. So right now, I feel like a ton of bricks were taken off my back, I thought he had a problem with the show or the band.

He invites me and Blake to sit down for a drink with him and the bunnies. And to be honest with you, I'm a little wired, because I just did a line of coke in the dressing room. But what the hell one drink ain't gonna kill me.

So we are sitting there having a drink, and one of the bunnies asked Blake what he did with the band. And Blake says to her, "I'm Doc's body guard". She looked at him and said "your awful small to be a body guard". Just then that stupid ass Blake reaches inside his coat, and pulls out a gun, and puts in right in her face and says, "This makes me the biggest mother fucker in here"

OK, now it's time to get the hell out of there, before we really fuck it up. But the manager was cool, and he walked me to the door as I was leaving, and apologized for the bunnie saying to Blake, that he looked too small to be a body guard. So a sticky situation that could have went a lot worst turned out OK, and the rest of the week went perfect. So perfect in fact, that we wound up performing in every Playboy club there was all over the world for the next year.

I could go on for pages on the tours, but I think it's time to move on to other subjects.

One of Doc Touring Bands With Myron Hale in the back and Larry Pasmore next to him

Doc On Tour In Newfoundland, Canada

Doc With Some of Members Of the Band

Doc With Blake Marean and Jimmy Derease (One of the guitar players)

Doc and Johnny Green from the Green Men Band in Newfoundland

Doc and a few of the Rabbits (Bunnies) at a Playboy Mansion party in LA

**Doc In Miami at the start
of the Playboy Club Tour**

Doc Holiday and Mike DeStefano in the Ducanes, Long Branch, New Jersey

**Doc and The JayWalkers
On The Jersey Shore**

Cissie Lynn
"The Forgotten One"

I guess, it was probably 30 or 35 years ago, from the time of the writing of this book, that I first met, the Daughter of the Coal Miners Daughter. That's right, country superstar Loretta Lynn's daughter, Cissie Lynn.

I met Cissie while I was living in Hampton Virginia. I was no longer touring at the time, and had settled into doing some record producing at a recording studio, I had opened up in town, called The Power Plant. I guess by that time I had really had my fill of performing live.

I had a very close friend in town named Bill, who owned a night club in town. He called me and told me that he got a call from Cissie Lynn, and she was looking for places that would hire her to sing. At the time I had no idea if she could sing or not, all I knew was, she was the daughter of Loretta Lynn and that had a lot of marquee value. So I told Bill, lets meet with her and see what she's got to offer.

So I guess it was about a week later, and she had driven up from Tennessee to Virginia to meet with us. At first meeting you could tell immediately that she was pure country, but I want to add right now that she was also a beautiful looking girl. Ah, but the big question still remained, can she sing? Well we were about to find that out because, Bill had hired her to sing in his club for one night.

I made sure that I went to the club that night to hear her, and she had a decent crowd that night, which proved what I said from the start, that name Lynn on the marquee would draw people.

Well she started her show set, and I tell you her band was the worst I had ever heard in my life, which I later found out that her boyfriend at the time put the band together, and to put it bluntly that band sucked. I was left wondering why such a superstars kid would go out with such a raggedy ass band, and you would think that her mother would intervene, and make sure that she went out as best as possible, not only to protect the name, but also to protect her daughter from public scrutiny.

Cissie finally came out to do her show, after that shitty band she had, played two songs and crucified everyone's ears in the club that night. Right from the first note that she sang, I knew that girl was special, and in my opinion for what ever that's worth, she was the best country voice, I ever heard in my life. I mean to tell you this girl had it all going on, she was pure country, and she could sing her ass off, plus on top of all that, she was a good-looking broad, and was the daughter of Loretta Lynn, talk about a triple knockout punch. This girl was a slam dunk, all she needed was to clean up her band and give her a little more polish, and she would be a pure moneymaker.

Well, I talked with her that night, and I agreed to take a ride down to a place called, Hurricane Mills, Tennessee, where she lived on the Loretta Lynn Ranch. I will say that me and her hit it off pretty good, because she was very sincere in convincing me, that she really wanted to be a singer. I mean she had the passion for it, and she felt she was born to do this, and there was no argument from me. In my eyes she was truly an undiscovered star, but I wanted to know more about her, before I committed to be involved in a career that involved another touring band.

So my wife and I jump in the car and we headed for Tennessee. At the time Cissie was living in a rundown single wide trailer with her daughter and son, and of course the boy friend, who I now found out, she had married him. Now, right off the bat, that struck me as being a little crazy. I mean here is this big ass mansion that Loretta Lynn lived in, and a mile away from the ranch, is her daughter living in, really for a better word, a shit hole. But little did I know, there were a whole lot of other surprises that would come to light.

So after Cissie made us lunch, we headed over to the big house, as she called it, to meet Loretta. When we got there, Cissie's father Mooney, was busy hooking up a 5th. wheel travel trailer to his pick up truck in the drive way, and Loretta was standing next to him.

Now you have to remember that this was before all the tourists and fans were on the ranch, to get a glimpse of Loretta Lynn. But, every once in a while, while we were standing in the driveway, a fan would drive by in a car, stop and look at the house, take a few pictures standing in the front of that archway, that was featured in the movie, The Coal Miners Daughter, and then stare at us all in the driveway, through the wrought iron fence that surrounded the house. I have to say, to me, it was a little uncomfortable seeing a group of fans standing about 100 feet away clamoring to get a look at Loretta. Funny thing though, it didn't seem to bother Loretta, Mooney or Cissie what so ever. But to me it was like living in a fishbowl.

At one point, there was probably a group of like 10 or 15 fans down by the fence, and Loretta actually walked down to the fence, and on her way down, she picked up a couple of small flat stones from the flower beds that lined the driveway, and believe it or not, she actually stood there and autographed those stones and gave them to the fans.

Well after spending some time with the Lynns, it became extremely clear to me, that Loretta was a down-home girl. But it also became very clear to me, that despite the image of being a simple country girl, she was also very aware that she was a country superstar, and although well hidden, there was also an ego, that would occasionally creep out and needed that Idol fix.

I want to make myself perfectly clear here, that I am not downgrading Loretta Lynn in any way. She is a superstar in country music, however I have come in contact with many country superstars, and no matter who they are, they all crave that attention, and have what I referred to as, a needed idol fix. And to put it bluntly they deserve it! It's part of the perks that you get, for all the hard work and sacrifices they have made, to achieve the notoriety and fame that they have acquired. And the key word in all of that is sacrifices, because whether you know it or not, I personally believe that any entertainer who achieves that level of greatness in the entertainment business, leaves a huge part of themselves behind,

That being said, it also appeared to me that of all the children Loretta had, I noticed that Cissie had a special place in her daddy's heart. I mean you could tell that every time that Mooney would look at her, or Cissie would speak, her dad had a very proud look on his face. It wasn't hard to tell that she was daddy's little girl, and by far his favorite, if it were possible to have a favorite with your children.

Okay now the burning question comes up once again. If that in fact is the case, then why is Cissie not getting the support she needed to achieve her goal as a country entertainer? Well as my relationship grew the answer became very clear to me, as you will see when we get further into the story. You have to always remember above all, there are two sides to every famous entertainer alive today. The one side, is the side that the public knows, and in most cases that side is fabricated by reporters, publicists and fans, who's goals and desires are, to create this sort of superhuman being, that never gets sick, never feels pain, never feels sorrow, and above all, never does anything wrong. And I have to admit that occasionally that entertainer can sometimes slip to a level where a big part of them, start to believe their own press. Not all of them now, but some of them have wound up in that whirlpool.

During my relationship with Cissie, I also noticed that there was a huge element of people who attempted to, and in many cases succeeded, in riding the coat tails of major superstars. I call them celebrity bloodsuckers, for lack of a better word or term. And in the case of the Lynns, these bloodsuckers were all over the place. But once again Mooney to the rescue. He kept that bullshit pretty much under control, and would occasionally step in and drain the swamp. I will say that Mooney ran a pretty tight ship when it came to the business end, and keeping that Idol fix and the real world of reality, under control as much as possible.

There was a saying at the time, "nothing goes on unless the man that lives in the big house on the hill says so", and that fact became very clear to everyone (including myself), involved in any way, shape or form, with the career of Loretta Lynn or her children.

Well, now that the meeting of the family was out-of-the-way, it was time to get down to the business at hand, and that business, was to make Cissie a country superstar.

The first thing that I had to address was her backup band. I mean in my opinion they were the worst I had ever heard, and fixing this problem would be a bigger obstacle that I had anticipated. You have remember that

I mentioned the celebrity bloodsuckers that surrounded Loretta. Well guess what folks, that nut didn't fall far from the tree, Cissie had them all over the place, and to cause a bigger problem some of them were actually in her so-called band, that had no talent what so ever, and was even living with Cissie. So get this now. We have a female backup singer in the band, who cannot sing a lick. Plus her husband is living at Cissie's with her and traveling with the band, and had no purpose whatsoever with the band other than draw a salary for doing nothing.

So, my first request was bluntly, fire those two immediately. A simple request to help further her career. But as I was about to find out, the request was not so simple. Cissie's husband at the time who claim to be "the band leader" (who by the way, we later found out, was nothing more than a Loretta Lynn groupie) wound up telling me there was no way he was going to fire those two. My response to him was "I'm not fuckin' telling you to, I'm telling her to do it, it's her career, not yours, and if she don't do it I will". Well needless to say I had my first roadblock, but if I was going to be successful in presenting Cissie Lynn at the best she could be, that I had to have control in fixing the obvious problems that was surrounding her, and those two members were nothing but a drain on the money she was making, and in the big picture, were extremely harmful to her performances.

It became blatantly clear that Cissie's husband was calling the shots, and that was probably the main reason she was failing in her attempt to achieve the level she needed to be at. You see Cissie's husband pictured himself as some sort of a future superstar in country music. And it was very clear that he was using Cissie's position as the daughter of Loretta, as a steppingstone for his own imaginary career. Unfortunately Cissie at the time failed to see that. And to make matters worse I later found out that he (the husband) had handpicked every member of her band, which all turned out to be friends of his. But at least now it was starting to show, why the support for Cissie's career was not in place as it should have been. Because not only did I see that, I am sure it was also seen at a higher level of the family support system.

So in short, I now had found one problem, but that problem could be fixed. That still did not fill my bucket with enough reasons to clarify why Cissie, was not getting the support and help she so desperately needed to achieve her goal from the family machinery. But as I said earlier, there were many other reasons that came into play, and as we get farther into the story you will see most of the reasons come to light.

Well it became clear, that there was no way possible, that I would win the case of eliminating the bloodsuckers that had attached themselves to the Cissie Lynn Gravy train. It seemed to me, that for some strange reason she did not have the conviction and courage to follow my instructions on that matter. I felt there was something strange going on behind the scenes, and for some reason she came across like a beaten puppy.

So I made the decision to back off on that band stuff, and cure the situation another way. There was no doubt about it, her husband John was pulling the strings and she was the puppet. But right now, my main focus was to get her working. I mean these people were not only taking advantage of her financially, but also mentally, and she was not able to see that. I remember her just sitting there staring at me unable or unwilling to voice her own opinion on what I was saying. But like I said, it was time to back off and concentrate on getting her out there performing.

My plan was to book her off the grid, in little small clubs in out-of-the-way places, where that sorry ass band could not hurt her, but in the meantime she would be gaining the experience of being able to work a crowd, and get polished as an entertainer.

So, I booked her on a Canadian tour of small clubs in out-of-the-way places, and that way I could kill two birds with one stone. Cissie would be making money that she needed badly, and she would gain the self-confidence and self-esteem that I felt she had been robbed of.

Before I sent her on the tour, she had met with me privately, to explain the financial crisis she was in. She told me jokingly "I can make spam a hundred different ways", and she had a big smile on her face when she said it.

I knew once, she got on the road she would see how these people were using her. Cissie may be a hillbilly, but, she ain't a dumb hillbilly. So it was time to leave Tennessee and get her on tour.

She probably performed in some of the

worst clubs you could imagine, but she did it like a trooper and never complained. The complaints were coming from her phoney ass husband, who was still trying to control every facet of the tour. I guess it was his way of justifying his existence. Well the tour ended and me and my wife, took another ride to Tennessee to meet with Cissie.

When we arrived, that shit hole single wide trailer she was living in, had now been replaced by a brand-new double wide trailer and it was pure luxury. I mean it had all the bells and whistles you could possibly imagine. No, it was not the big house on the hill, but she was finally moving in the right direction. The bottom line was, she was now making money, and even though the bloodsuckers were still there draining her, she made the decision to better her living situation. I was very proud of her, she had gone out there and got the job done, and was now starting to feel better about herself, and that was important to me.

I can remember my wife asking me, "do you really think she is that good of a singer", and my answer was "of all my years doing music, she is the best traditional country singer I ever heard"," if anybody in this whole

God Damn crew of siblings has a shot, she, without a doubt is the rightful heir to the Loretta Lynn throne". I meant that then, and I still mean it today. The bottom line is, Cissie never really knew how damn good she was. And that I would find out, would be one of the biggest things that kept her always, on the sidelines and not getting the support of the Loretta Lynn machinery. She was so good she was conceived to be a threat to the dynasty. You remember I told you there were to sides to every superstar. The public side and the private side, and make no mistake about it, that private side, and in many cases, has an ego.

So here we are in Hurricane Mills meeting with Cissie and discussing the last tour. Cissie suggested that we go over to her mother's house (Loretta), and of course I agreed, because I wanted to dig deeper, and find out if Cissie could get some support, due to the success of this last tour she did.

So we get in my car, and I thought we were just going down the road to the big house. I had no idea that Cissie was talking about going to see her mother, in Loretta's Nashville house. Anyway, we started to make the two-hour drive from Hurricane Mills to

Nashville. However, the good part of this trip, was Cissie's husband John, was not with us, it was just me, my wife and Cissie. I think by now, that John realized that I had no use for his ass or his friends, so he was in a way throwing a little pity party for himself, which did not faze me in the least bit.

We finally arrived at the house in Nashville, and the three of us walked in and there was Loretta sitting on the couch with her back towards us watching television. Cissie walked in and said "Mama do you remember Doc Holiday"? Loretta turned around and said "of course I do", and said to me "come over here Doc and give me some sugar". So I walked over and gave her a kiss on the cheek, just then Mooney came out of the kitchen and said, "Doc, you want some breakfast"? And I'm thinking at this point, old Mooney is gonna whip up a serious southern style breakfast, you know, country ham, biscuits and grits. So I looked at Mooney and said "hell yea", and then Mooney went back into the kitchen.

Just then Loretta got up and said to my wife," come here I want to show you something", and she proceeded to take my wife and Cissie into another room, that was actually converted into a huge walk-in closet. I mean when she opened the door there was nothing but wall to wall clothes. So while Loretta was in there, busy giving my wife a bunch of clothes from a new clothing line that Loretta was going to develop. You know, shirts, and blouses.

Now I walked back into the kitchen with Mooney, I mean I am ready for this southern style breakfast. Mooney is sitting at the table in a chair with his legs crossed, you know, Indian style. He looks at me and in front of him was a loaf of bread, a jar of peanut butter, and another jar of jelly. He again looked at me and said "how much peanut butter you want on this son bitch". Okay, there goes my dreams of a southern style breakfast, a peanut butter and jelly sandwich.

So while Mooney is fixing up his culinary delight, he looks at me and says "where's Loretta". And I said, she's in that room, giving my wife a bunch of clothes. And now comes the most classic line of all time. And really, I should not be sharing this with anyone, because it was said in private. Mooney leaned over to me and said in a whisper, "she ain't nothing, Doc, but a hillbilly that got lucky", (I guess they were feuding a little that day and, it has been rumored that Mooney would take a little sip of the moonshine from time to time). But I came right back and said jokingly "no Mooney, your, the hillbilly that got lucky". He just gave me a big smile and went on preparing that award winning peanut butter and jelly sandwich.

Okay, now the picture was becoming very clear to me. There was definitely family love in play, however, when it came to anything that had to do with the entertainment business, would come up, all rules went out the window. It was like, the old story, "Hey, I love you BUT this is business!", Now in some sort of weird way, I was able to see why the lack of support, was blatantly missing when it came to Cissies career.

There was a moment, that kind of brought a smile to my face, while I was sitting at the table with Mooney. Me and Cissie had just finished a demo recording, of Cissie singing the first cut of the song, Letter to Loretta, and if I do say so myself, it was a pretty damn good demo.

I had with me that day a small portable CD player, and I played the demo for Mooney. We sat and listened to the whole song, and in typical Mooney fashion, he looked up and said with a smile "you need to put a damn, banjo on that". It was later that I found out, that Mooney wanted a banjo on every God damn song he heard.

Well the visit came to an end Nashville, and we headed back to Hurricane Mills, and I have to say that this visit clarified a lot of doubts and suspicions that were in a way connected to the journey, myself and Cissie were on. But, I could also see that this career thing was going to be, one hell of a ride.

I knew it was now time for me to dig a little bit deeper and find out, why that family support for Cissie's career, was not rushing out like the dam in front of the big house had just broke. I will admit, it did not take a whole lot of searching to see the big picture that was forming. Case in point. The oldest daughter of Loretta Lynn, Betty Sue Lynn, was an extremely talented songwriter, and in reality her mother Loretta had recorded four of the songs that Betty Sue had written. Wine women and song, Before I'm over you, The other woman, and finally, The home your tearin' down. But for some reason, Loretta stopped recording songs that Betty Sue had written. Well it wasn't hard to figure out why.

It seemed that Betty Sue had written a song call Ole Rooster, and Mooney loved the song. Cissie told me one day that Mooney had said to Loretta, "Betty Sue writes better songs, than you do". Well that did it, Mooney had inadvertently signed Betty Sue's death certificate, when it came to writing songs for Loretta. You always have to remember that the private side of the stars ego is extremely fragile. Well in short it was now becoming evident, that maybe just maybe, our little girl Cissie was not the only forgotten one in the Lynn dynasty. It seemed everything was cool, and it's great, if you get in the business, but don't try to take the throne or the crown too soon, and on your own. It seemed Loretta's coat tails were not very long and were not easy to ride;

Betty Sue passed away and unfortunately she never received the credit and accolades she deserved for her brilliant songwriting. Make no mistake about it she was one hell of a songwriter,

Now the facts started to jump out, and the road that me and Cissie had to travel, to achieve the success that Cissie rightfully deserved, would prove to be full of potholes. And we both now faced the fact, that we would have to do it on our own. And do we did! I started work on booking another tour, and this one was going to be huge. A six month tour, the big question was, could she, (Cissie), stand the pressure. There was only one way to find out, Cissie, pack your bags you're going on tour, Lynn kid.

No big surprise here, Cissie went out and she was a smash hit in everyplace she performed. There was no stopping her now, she would make a ton of money, everything was going great, But, you know it's like that old saying, "nothing good last forever".

I got a phone call one day while Cissie was out on the road, from a club owner she had just performed in. He told me how great she did and how the people loved her. But he also gave me some bad news. He informed me, that Cissie's husband John, had attempted to book the band, without Cissie, back into the club, changing the name of the band from the Coal Dusters to the Busted Cowboy Band. And of course the husband would be the main attraction.

I did not say a word to Cissie about it, but when the tour was completed, I got John to the side and said "you pull that shit one more fuckin' time mother fucker, and I will bury your ass". Of course, his lying ass denied it, he claimed that the club owner approached him to buy the band back without Cissie. Which I knew was a bunch of bullshit. That confrontation with him started to unravel the whole journey that we were on. Her husband now knew, that I saw through him like a dirty piece of glass.

I never told Cissie about that, but probably when she reads this book, will be the first she has ever heard of it. But I figured bringing it up back then was a losing battle, because after all he had her conned to the point of believing that he was her knight in shining armor. Plus then, there started a lot of turmoil that was starting at the ranch, and Cissie was about to get sucked into it.

Remember I told you Mooney ran a very tight ship, when it came to Loretta's business. There was actually a time when Loretta, had her son Ernest, traveling with her, and opening up for her at her shows. Back in those days Ernie was a wild man, always getting into trouble. Loretta once told me "he's meaner than a snake". Well it got so bad, that Mooney actually fired him. That's right, you heard me right, Mooney fired Ernie.

I guess Mooney woke up one morning,

and decided to drain the swamp, and Ernie was the first casualty. But there was more to come. There was a guy called Tim, that traveled with Loretta and did her hair. Well, to put it bluntly Mooney didn't care for this character very much, he told Loretta "you tell that son of a bitch, I don't want him in my house". And from that day forward Tim never went in the house again, he would just go straight up to the bus, and wait there to leave on tour. Like I said, Mooney ran a tight ship, when it came to people, he felt were bloodsuckers, just hanging onto Loretta for a paycheck.

Things were about to get a lot worse, Mooney got deathly sick, and Cissie was at his bedside every minute of every day. The bottom line was, Cissie was daddy's little girl, and everybody on that ranch knew it.

Mooney passed away and all hell broke loose. Celebrity bloodsuckers came out of the woodwork. One day after Mooney had died, Tim the hairdresser moved into the house, Ernie went back on the road opening for Mama, Cissie's husband John informed me that he was now going to start to manage the band and Cissie, and no longer needed me to do it. I want to say right now, and

I mean this from the bottom of my heart "WITHOUT DOOLITTLE MOONEY" LYNN, THERE WOULD NOT BE A LORETTA LYNN. And you could take that to the bank!

I did not argue the point in any way, shape or form. It was getting too crazy for me, and as much as I cared for her, I knew it was time, to throw in the towel. I knew that eventually Cissie would see the light, and just for the record, I did not see Cissie or Loretta for the next 15 years. Then I got a call from out of the blue, and it was Cissie telling me she wanted to sing again.

It seems that John drove her into bankruptcy and she had lost everything, but the biggest thing, and the greatest thing that she had lost was, she divorced his ass finally!!! It took her 15 years to figure it out, but she finally got it right. But unfortunately she was past her prime, and it was too late start over again.

Today, me and Cissie remain very close, or at least we were until she reads this book. Sorry Lynn kid, but I had to tell it the way it really was.

DOC, CISSIE, DOC'S WIFE JUDY AND LORETTA AT THE BIG HOUSE ON THE HILL

(BY THE WAY LORETTA MADE MOONEY TAKE THIS PICTURE)

**DOC AND CISSIE IN AN
EARLY STUDIO DEMO SESSION**

**25 YEARS LATER DOC AND CISSIE
AT QUAD STUDIOS, NASHVILLE, TN.**

CISSIE AND DOC IN 2015 ON THE FRONT PORCH IN HURRICANE MILLS, TN.

DOC WITH THE SECOND GENERATION OF COUNTRY MUSIC ROYALTY

(LORETTA'S DAUGHTER, CISSIE LYNN)

(HANK WILLIAMS SR. DAUGHTER, JETT WILLIAMS)

**MOONEY LYNN HOOKIN' UP THE 5TH WHEEL
MOONEY IN THE DRIVEWAY
OF THE BIG HOUSE**

**DOC & CISSIE ACTING FOOLISH ON THE
FRONT PORCH OF THE BIG HOUSE**

Same Song, Different Places, Different Faces

I'm sure you all heard that saying, "it's that same old song again", or "same shit different day", and of course my favorite that I used all the time, "Same old shit, just comin' from different fuckin' directions". Well I guess that holds a lot of truth in many cases, but, the changing faces, the different places, somehow makes that same old song different.

As you all get to know me on a more personal level, through this book, you may find it hard to believe, that so many people and places, came into play during my life time.

But I assure you, every single word, everyplace I mentioned, and every person mentioned in this memoir, is well documented and truthful to the smallest detail, no matter how hard, and how revealing it may all seem.

I can look back and remember, so many different recording studios that I worked in, and the many nightclubs and concerts that I performed in, that were too numerous to mention, and in so many different places, today it all seem to run together. And when you really analyze it all, no matter where how or where it took place, it all seemed like the same shit over and over. But when it was happening it was totally a different ballgame, with different challenges and different mountains to move, but in most cases the rewards and final outcomes, seem to make it all worthwhile at the time.

One of the many "Stars" that crossed my path was, BAM MARGERA. At the time my youngest daughter Carmela, was a huge fan of Bam, because he had a television show, that was on MTV called, Viva La Bam, where he did all kinds of crazy shit. Plus he was doing all the "Jackass" movies with Johnny Knoxville, so he was hotter than a firecracker at the box office.

So one day, I get a call from Bam's manager "Tim", asking me if I could meet with Bam, because he is going to be in Norfolk, Virginia, touring with a band he is sponsoring called "Him". Well I wasn't really doing anything that night, so I said what the hell, plus the fact my daughter would love to meet him.

So I gave my daughter a call and said, " I have to go to the Norva tomorrow night, how would you like to go backstage and meet Bam?". Well, to say she went crazy would put it lightly. I really never had second thoughts about her meeting him, because I thought the character he played on television was actually that, a character, and not really who he was. Anyone who ever saw his show or his movies would know, this guy was one crazy son of a bitch. But being in the entertainment business my whole life, I knew, or at least I thought I knew, that this was his act, you know acting that crazy. WELL I WAS WRONG, THIS WAS ONE CRAZY MOTHER FUCKER.

Well we got to the Norva that night, and the place was sold out. We were led backstage by one of the security guards, and seated in a room, and told, Bam would be right in.

My daughter was so excited, she had brought with her a skateboard for him to sign, oh yea, I forgot to tell you that he was also a famous skateboarder at the time. There were about eight other people in the room, I guess they were all waiting for Bam. Just then there he was, walking into the doorway with his entourage, and four guys with video cameras taking video of every move he made. I guess this was the MTV crew.

We were sitting well to the rear of the room, when he walked in, of course the people that were sitting toward the door, got up and crowded around him to get an autograph. He signed a few autographs and shook a few hands, and then I noticed he looked up, and spotted us sitting in the back of the room, away from the crowd, and said his goodbyes to the fans, and walked up to the table that we were sitting at. At that time his road manager introduced him to me by saying, "Bam, this is Doc Holiday", he smiled, and shook my hand. I said "Bam, this is my daughter Carmela", he turned around and stuck his hand out and said "Hi, Bam Margera."

Right now I have to tell you that my daughter had met some of the most famous people in the entertainment Industry, and never acted starstruck in any way, but when Bam spun around and suck out his hand, she for the first time, totally lost it.

Well we sat around for probably close to two hours just shooting the shit, and my daughter, Carmela, was in her glory. The cameras were rolling all the time, she was smiling ear to ear, and she got him to autographed every possible thing on that table, from napkins, to coasters and of course a thing she still cherishes today, that skateboard.

So I guess you're all wondering right now was all that craziness an act. Well I'm here to tell you the answer to that question is absolutely HE WAS A PURE NUT CASE!, Bam was exactly the way he was on television and in the movies. He is a complete crazy ball of energy, going full blast all the time, and never letting up. I mean he wore me out just watching him, and the bottom line was, I liked him! He was different, and definitely talented, he could handle himself in any situation. So all in all, I'm glad I went to that meeting, and most of all my daughter made a memory that she will remember her whole life.

Doc's Daughter Carmela and Bam

Doc Holiday and Bam, Backstage

Enter Kevin Costner, Academy award winning actor, known throughout the world, and now has decided to try his luck at becoming a country singer. That's right, you heard me correct, Kevin had recorded a country album, and formed a touring band called, Modern West.

Kevin had requested a meeting with me through his management company, and of course I jumped at the chance, because I was a huge fan of him and all his movies.

The night that we went to meet him, I brought along my friend, Red Hawk, and of course my wife Judy. Red Hawk came along because of the movie Kevin had made called, "Dancing With Wolves". To be honest with you, I myself have loved every movie that he ever put out . I thought he was brilliant as an actor, and I wanted to ask him, how he went about choosing the scripts, because like I said, I had never saw him in a bad movie.

The night that we all went to meet him, Kevin was performing a concert, and we were going to meet backstage before his show. We got to the room where we were supposed to meet, and there had to be two dozen middle aged women standing outside the room, to get a small glimpse of their idol.

Well a security guard arrived, and led us past the line of fans gathered outside the room. As the door opened up to the room, everyone could see a small glimpse of Kevin, standing in the middle of the room, and I will tell you now, that small glimpse of him, drove those women into a frenzy, to where you would think they were a bunch of teenagers .

We entered the room and Kevin came over to greet us. My first impression? Believe it or not, I noticed he had very little hair on the top of his head, and in every movie I ever saw him in, he always had a very full head of hair, (Welcome to Hollywood, where I guess nothing is real). But needless to say he was still a good-looking guy, and it was easy to see why he was a chick magnet.

After we all introduced ourselves, we got into some great conversation. I remember asking him of all the movies that he had been in, which was his favorite. Now you have to remember, I had Red Hawk with me that night, and Hawk was looking very Native American as he always did. Kevin told us of all the roles he ever had, he said he wanted Dancing With Wolves the most. And I was surprised when he told us, that he was raise as a child by his grandmother who was a full blooded Native American and lived on a reservation. I had no idea that he was brought up in that kind of environment. So needless to say, him and Red Hawk, bonded quickly.

I can recall telling Kevin that year that, I was on the nominating committee for the Grammy awards, and if his album came down the pike, he could count on my support. I figured in some way, that was the reason I was offered the meeting with him. However he came right back and said "Doc, I could care less about awards, I just really want to sing", and he was serious when he said that.

Well the meeting lasted one hour or more, and it was time for Kevin to go on stage, and do his concert. So the three of us were given VIP seats to see the show, but before he left, he asked if we would like to get some pictures together for a memory. Of course we all agreed and proceeded one by one to take a picture with Kevin. My wife Judy, was the last one to take a picture with him, I will never forget that moment. They stood side by side, Kevin put his arm around her, and she put her arm around his waist, and looked up at him and said "I never realized you were this skinny", he smile and said to her, "now that's cute"

We saw the concert that night, and I have to say, he put on one hell of a show.

Doc Holiday and Kevin Costner Back Stage

Ladies and Gentlemen, Tiny Tim.

I first saw Tiny in Greenwich Village New York, in the mid-60's. He was working at a club, I think it was called the black pussycat, now I could be wrong about that, but if memory serves me right I believe that was the name.

Ok, now here is this guy standing on stage, with long ass hair playing a ukulele, and singing like a canary. To say it was odd would be an understatement, but then again there was a lot of odd shit going on in the village, during that time period. So in reality, he kind of in a strange way fit in, or should I say, blended in with that whole hippie movement that was taking place throughout Greenwich Village.

I'm going to move forward about 10 years, when I was on tour, and watching television while on a break. The show was called, Laugh-In, and it was pretty popular at the time. Then all of a sudden, here's this guy on the show, singing a Sonny and Cher song, I got you babe. As soon as I saw him, I remember, this was a guy I saw in the village, and what brought it all back to me was, he was singing both parts, the male part and the female part. I can remember thinking back then, that this was all a very big act, I mean really, nobody could be that fucked up right? It had to be an act. Thinking back, I remember telling my band mates, "hey, you guys remember that freak we saw down at the village, you know the one that played a ukulele and sounded like he had he had his balls in a vice grip". "Well that son of a bitch is on national television, doing that same shit".

It was about a year or so later that he had a huge hit record titled,"Tiptoe through the Tulips". I mean to tell you that damn record sold millions of copies, and here we are busting our balls, trying to come up with a great song, so we could get a record out there. And here comes this guy with a routine and act like he was from another planet, and he's selling millions of records, on national television to boot. I mean really, was the public actually buying this crap, it was clearly all an act. But buy it they did, and this guy became a worldwide phenomenon. Little did I know that this guy on television, playing that ukulele and singing like a bird, would play a major part in my life story.

Now we turn the clock ahead about five or six years. I'm performing in a club in Florida called Da Vinci's, located very near Cocoa Beach. The owner of this club was named Marty, and he actually owned two clubs in that area. The one we were working at, was more of a night club. The other club that he owned, was a strip club called The Cork Club. Well anyway one night Marty comes up to me, and said, "Doc, I just booked Tiny Tim to do a show at the Cork Club". I was totally blown away. I said "are you fuckin' nuts"? He had a big smile on his face and then handed me the contract, and surer then shit, there it was, he booked Tiny Tim to do a show in this club with the strippers.

So anyway I started to read his rider for

the engagement. Now most entertainers, will put in their rider what they need to do the performance, you know like, special equipment on stage, certain kind of lighting, and stuff like that. Well I'm reading Tiny's rider, and this is what he needed to do the show. He wanted of course, a motel room, plus ground transportation to and from the club. Now it starts to get a little weird, the rider states he wanted a baseball pin ball machine in the motel room, plus 2 rolls of dimes, wait, wait, you ain't gonna believe this shit, he wants a huge bowl of spaghetti, with nothing but butter on it, no sauce Just Butter!. So right now I have been thinking all along, that this guy, Tiny Tim, was a total fake act, I mean really folks, nobody could be that weird. But now I am having second thoughts, because this rider is fuckin' nuts.

Now I must tell you that Tiny's career had taken a huge nose dive, and he was playing the little 200 and 300 seat clubs for peanuts. Anyway he still had a huge name and that name could draw people. So what if it was a freak show, he still had marquee drawing power.

It's showtime, the place Is sold out, and my band is going to be the back up band for

Tiny. Now mind you we have had no rehearsal with him at all, and the only thing that I can remember about him was his hit, Tiptoe through the Tulips. Marty had Tiny in his office, so there was no way that we could get together and figure out what songs he would going to do.

Well to make a long evening shorter, he comes walking out of the office, with his ukulele in one hand and a shopping bag in the other hand. He jumped right on stage with no introduction, puts his shopping bag on the floor, and just starts to sing. My band had no idea what the hell he was doing, or what songs he was singing. So they're trying to follow him, the songs he was singing just ran into each other, there was no break it was continuous, and to top it all off, I, as well as everybody else in the audience had no clue what the hell these songs were. (I later found out there all songs of the 1800's, it seems that Tiny was a big fan of songs that were written in the 17 and 1800's.

Needless to say at this point it became embarrassing, and you can even see the tension on the people in the audience, they were totally bewildered by what was taking place on the stage in front of them.

My band wound up walking off the stage after about six minutes, because there was no way that they could follow what this guy was doing, and it should be noted that Tiny never stopped singing, but we got through the night and Tiny put on his show, good or bad, it was definitely a show. At the end, he picked up his shopping bag and retreated back into the office.

I went back to the office to meet him, and when I got back there, it was more shocking than what I had seen on stage. I mean here he is, sitting behind the desk, still with a ukulele in hand, and Marty introduced me by saying, "Tiny, this is Doc Holiday". Tiny stands up and in a very timid voice says, "oh Mr. Holiday it is such an honor and a pleasure to finally meet you". Right now I'm thinking what the fuck is happening here. The guy had probably a quarter of an inch of cold cream all over his face. I swear there was no way to see his skin, he was totally covered with cold cream. And to boot he was moving around the office, like a butterfly, and sounding like one too.

So in short this was the guy that sold 8 million records, and was known throughout the world, and what I thought for the past five or six years, the guy that was putting on an act, it started to become apparently real to me, that this was no act. What you saw on stage was the real deal. I thought to myself this guy is not human, he's like from another planet. I mean whoever walked in the office, this guy was blowing kisses to people and totally acting off-the-wall. Just then somebody wanted to take a picture of me and him, so I did the customary side by side pose, and Marty said to me, ". Doc, do me a favor and give Tiny a ride back to the motel'. I'm saying to myself holy shit, I got a ride in the car with this fuckin' guy,

Well I agreed to do it, and me and Tiny get in the car for the drive back to the motel. Now you have to understand the motel was about 45 minutes away from the club, which gave us more than enough time to have a conversation. I'm telling you right now believe it or not, this guy was no fake. That freak you saw on stage was exactly who he was. There was no act whatsoever. I mean really, how does a human being get that fucked up.

So we were driving, and we are having a conversation about everything you can ever imagine, I mean this guy could talk, and I might add he could talk about a million different subjects, and he was extremely knowledgeable on all of them. Really this guy was no dummy, he was smart as hell, but he was also weirder than shit.

I remember there was a moth, flying around inside the car, and I went to smash it against the windshield, and he panicked, not because of the moth, because I was going to kill it. I pulled the car over and opened the door and the moth flew away. And for five minutes all he kept saying was " thank you Mr. Holiday, thank you Mr. Holiday", You know you've heard the statement he wouldn't kill a fly, well in Tiny's case, trust me he wouldn't kill a fly.

While I finally got him back to his motel, and asked him if he had transportation to the airport in the morning, and he responded, "oh yes, Mr Marty is going to pick me up". I noticed when I was standing in his motel room and I didn't see any clothes hanging up or any luggage. I asked him where his luggage was, and I would take it with me, and give it to Marty, so he had it when he picked him up in the morning. That's when he informed me that he had no luggage, everything he needed was in that shopping bag. Just when you thought it couldn't get any weirder, it did.

Well I said my goodbyes and figured

I would never see Tiny again, I couldn't be any more wrong, because 11 months later I would be booked to go on tour with him, and was told that he specifically asked for me and my band, to do this Canadian tour, which would last 13 weeks. Well the money was good, so I agreed to do it.

Well, we are all off to Canada. The band is leaving from Alabama, and I am leaving from Miami, and we are going to meet in a place call Moncton, New Brunswick. As I am driving up on Interstate 95, I pulled over for coffee in South Carolina, at a place called South of the Border. I called my agent to let them know we were all on our way up, and then he hit me with the news, that I have to make a stop in Boston Massachusetts, to pick up Tiny. It seems that my agent agreed that we would supply all ground transportation for this tour. Right about now, you're probably wondering why the hell I agreed to do this tour in the first God Damn place. It was real simple, money. There was a total of 19 dates booked, and my band would get $10,000 per player, and I would walk away with $62,000 net, and for that kind of money, if they told us it was in the North Pole, are ass's would have been there.

So I make it to Boston and pick up Tiny, and start heading to New Brunswick Canada, where the first show was at a place called the Urban Cowboy. This journey into nowhere land starts the minute I get Tiny. He gets into the car with absolutely no luggage, all he got is a God damn shopping bag and his fucking ukulele. But the best is yet to come, I'm going to be sitting in a car with this guy for the next 20 hours.

We finally make it to the Maine, Canadian border, and it's like 3 AM in the morning. Now you can just imagine the faces on the immigration people at the border when Tiny stepped out of the God damn car. Oh I forgot to mention he was wearing a tuxedo with tales that was made up of hundreds of Mickey Mouse figures all over it. You heard me right, the tuxedo was white with hundreds of multicolored Mickey Mouse drawings all over it. That freak show had begun, but to my surprise I was the only one freaking out, the border guards were all rushing to get his autograph, and finally after a one hour delay, because of him signing autographs, we crossed the border into Canada.

We arrived in Moncton, checked into the hotel rooms, and I met with my band who had arrived a day earlier. They told me that the club was a 700 seater and was sold out, and I said "cool, lets get this fucking circus on the road".

I'm going to try and condense this whole tour and to just a few paragraphs, but believe me this tour would have enough going on to write another damn book. Well we did the show that night, and by the way, Tiny is still wearing the same tuxedo with the Mickey Mouse all over it, only now once again his face is totally covered in cold cream. But ironically enough the crowd fuckin' loved him. Makes you want to just scratch your head and say, what the hell is this world coming to.

Anyway we pack up and head off to the next date. For the next seven or eight dates, it was basically the same shit every night, and the strangest part of the whole deal was, they loved him on every show, and on every show it took us 1 to 2 hours to get the hell out of there, because Tiny insisted on signing autographs for everyone that wanted one of them.

By now you figured out, that me and Tiny spent a lot of time in the car together going from show to show. One time we got on the conversation of when he did the Johnny Carson show and got married to Miss Vicki on the show. That Tonight Show, wound up being the highest rating show of all the Tonight Shows ever. And Tiny informed me, that he got stuck in Los Angeles, because NBC would not pay for his hotel room, and he and Miss Vicki had absolutely no money on them whatsoever. So get this, the guy pulled in the highest rating of all the Tonight Shows, they pay his manager $320 for his appearance (which was the union scale at the time) and they stiff him on the motel room. But nonetheless his manager paid the hotel bill the next morning. That's when I found out why Tiny never had any money on him. It seemed that this manager that he had, who by the way was the same manager he had for the past 15 years, only paid him $250 a week. You heard me right, at the peak of his career, when he was making hundreds of thousands of dollars, all he ever got paid from the manager was $250 a week. Talk about getting fucked, they were using this guy to no end, and he had no clue what was taking place.

Well by the time we were almost through with the tour, I had really gotten to understand, the real Tiny Tim. He was basically so nice and so giving, and he never questioned anything as long as he was allowed to keep singing. He didn't care about money, in his eyes everything was beautiful, every flower that he saw was awesome and even bugs had a place on this planet. It was a shame what they had done to him, the way they screwed him over, but hey welcome to fuckin' show business.

We finished the tour, and I remember driving Tiny back to Massachusetts, and before I dropped him off, I had an envelope that I had put together, with eight thousand dollars in it, because I knew, that they were not going to give him any money whatsoever. So when we pulled up to the place that he was staying at, before he got out of the car, I gave him the envelope, and I said Tiny this is for you. And in his innocence, he thought it was a goodbye card. He opened the envelope, and saw 80, one hundred dollar bills, and he said, " Mr. Holiday, (he never addressed me any other way than Mr. Holiday), what is all this money for? I said ",Tiny I know they're only going to give you like $400 or $500 for this whole tour, and you did a really great job, and this is just my way of saying thanks.

He would not take the money, because

like I said he never really did what he did for the money, he did it because in his mind he was entertaining, and bringing happiness to his fans, and that's all he ever really cared about. He had a beautiful soul, too beautiful for this fucked up business we are in.

I never got a chance to work with Tiny or to speak with him again, but I had heard through the Grapevine, that he was still touring, but had gained a lot of weight and had a heart attack. He survived the heart attack, but was told by his doctors to lose weight, and to not continue performing for at least three months. Tiny, of course did not, and of course would not follow those orders, and a week later, he was performing at a show, and felt sick halfway through the show. His current wife at the time, begged him to cut the show short, but his response was, "I must sing my hit song, that's what they came to hear".

Tiny Tim had a massive heart attack that night, and died on the stage singing, Tiptoe through the Tulips. He was unable to finish his song and really, that's all he ever lived for.

Tiny Tim and Doc Holiday

Well I have to say there were tons of on tour stories, but I guess it will have to go into a third book to get it all in.

There was the Jan and Dean tour when they were riding the charts up in the top five, with that record, Little Old Lady From Pasadena. There was a lot of shit that went down on that tour, to be honest with you, there was so much cocaine involved, that most of it is a blur. I'll get into that another time.

Then of course there was the Waylon Jennings, Roger Miller tour, and that was actually a lot of fun. I remember one backstage story from that tour. It was myself, Waylon and Roger sitting backstage before the show started, and Roger had just smoked a joint. Waylon asked Roger, "how was that dope?, Roger said, "it was really good man, I mean really good". Waylon came right back with "how high did it get you", and Roger who was really fuckin' stone said, " high enough to go duck hunting with a rake ".

I guess that says it all right there, and like I said I could go on for years just doing road stories, but I have to move on otherwise this book will become as long as war and peace.

Different Studios, Same Bullshit

You know during my career, I have been in over 1000 recording studios. Some were small home studios in a garage or basement, some were in warehouse complexes or strip shopping centers, some were freestanding buildings and some were million-dollar studios. And to be perfectly honest with you, when you get to that level of a $1 million studio, they all are basically the same. I mean sure they look different, but as far as the equipment is concern they are all pretty much basically the same. The bottom line is really not the equipment but, the person behind the equipment. For an example you can buy a $7000 keyboard, and put a player on it that doesn't know his ass from a hole in the ground, and that keyboard will sound like shit. Take the same keyboard and put a hall of fame musician on it, and it sounds like a million bucks. So in short, it's not the equipment, it ain't the building, and it sure as hell ain't the location. It is, and always has been, the players and the people involved in running the session, it's that simple.

You know there is an old saying about someone arrested and going to trial, and it goes like this. A defendant that represents himself in court, has a fool for a client. That saying can also be used in the recording industry, however it goes something like this. An artist who produces himself, is a fucking moron. It is the producers job to know what the public, labels and radio, is buying at that particular time in the industry. Bottom line is, you could have the sweetest apples in the world, but if the record companies and public is buying peaches, your fucked! That is one of the main reasons you have a producer in the first damn place. It's not for the artist to tell the producer what he wants the record to sound like, it's for the producer to tell the artist what the record should sound like, in order for it to be successful in the industry. That's why it's so important to pick the right producer.

Case in point, so many of these so-called record producers in Nashville, give you this shit, " I worked with this, and that superstar 25 years ago". Well guess what, don't tell me what the fuck you did, tell me what you're doing now, and in most cases that will be a real short conversation.

Well, as of the writing of this book, I now limit all my productions to a place call Sony studios in Nashville, Tennessee. But actually my career as a producer didn't start there in Nashville, it started way before that, many years ago, but right now I'll concentrate on the Nashville part of my career.

I guess it was about 20 or 25 years ago, I went into a studio in the Nashville area called Bradley s Barn. It was owned by a guy they called the architect of country music, Owen Bradley. It was at the barn, that really became the first birthplace of what is now known as Country Music and also happens to be where Doc Holiday's Studio "A" Team was born. And really it all came together quite by accident. It started at an event that was a yearly thing in Nashville call Fan Fare. It was there that I ran into a guy who was circulating through the crowd, handing out his business cards. It seems he was a guitar player who had just relocated to Nashville from Los Angeles, and was trying to get his name out in the country music community. His name is Dale Herr, and I didn't know it then, but he would become a major part and player in my career for the next 20 to 25 years as a record producer.

It seemed that Dale had an extensive background and a huge amount of success in Los Angeles, however during that time, it didn't mean shit, when it came to the Nashville music scene. You see back then, Nashville was still controlled by the good old boys, and if you weren't in that little click, then your success would be extremely limited. That being said, I inadvertently fell in to the Mecca of country music when I entered Bradly's Barn. I didn't know it then, but that studio in the middle of a bunch of farmland just outside of Nashville, would cause my career to take a major left turn, and would stay on that path, for the rest of my career as a producer. But looking back at it now, trust me, that was a good thing.

It should be noted at this time, you have to remember I was a New Jersey, New York guy which was totally a different scene and atmosphere, from that country setting and laid-back hillbilly attitude. To be honest with you, I hated that city. I mean I didn't like the people, I didn't like the town, in short I didn't like any part of it, but for some reason I formed a very quick bond with the people that were involved in the studio that very first day.

The engineer for the day was a guy called, Bobby Bradley. To say he was knowledgeable would be an understatement, it became quickly apparent, that he was brilliant at what he was doing on the recording console, but then again why shouldn't he be, he was taught by the guy that created country music in Nashville, Owen Bradley.

On the first night at the barn, I walked into the studio, and the first person I saw was the bass player sitting on a chair. I remember asking Dale," is this guy any good?", And Dale responded "his name is Dave Roe, and he's been with Johnny Cash playing bass for the past 15 years". Well that was good enough for me. Then came the drummer, he had long gray hair, and sure as hell did not look like a country music player. I spent a little time talking to him, and discovered that he had played on almost every hit record recorded in Nashville. His name was Craig Krampf. Oh yea, remember I told you he did not look like a country music player. While I found out that night , the he was also the co writer for Steve Perry's "big hit, "Oh Sherry", with the band Journey. So once again that was cool with me, I mean we had some serious, serious, players in that studio that night.

So you see, it was really quite by accident that we all came together, on that first night at the Barn, and in reality that was the actual birth of what is now known as Doc Holiday's legendary studio "A" team in Nashville recording circles. And the strangest part of the whole first session was, we all stayed together on every single session that I produced after that night for the next 20 years. Along the way we added some people, and we replaced some people, but that nucleus has been together like I said, for the past 20 years, and I have never done a recording session without them since that first night at the barn.

Along the way we added players like Jim Horn who was a legendary saxophone player, and a guitar player Jim Boyd (who has since passed away), and of course when we needed a fiddle player, who else but the legendary Ragin' Cajun Doug Kershaw, and when David was busy on the road we had Garry Tallent, from Bruce Springsteen's E St. band, jump in and filled the spot. The Deb Thomas singers where there right from the start, doing all the background vocals. And if I ever needed a female lead singer to do a part, I was always fortunate enough to get a Nashville icon by the name of Becky Hobbs. So in short what you see there, is what you're going to see every time I walk into a studio to produce a record. But I will say right now that Dale and Bobby became my safety net. Those two guys were the ones I leaned on the most to get it done. And they are still to this day the guys I count on the most. I never have to check on those guys. I tell him what I need one time, and I never have to ask them again if they got it done. They are professionals at the highest level, as well as every member of that team, and to be honest with you, a lot of my success is because of that team.

Doc Holiday "A" Team at Quad Studios, Nashville, TN. Bobby Bradley. Jim Boyd, Doc Holiday, Dave Roe, Dale Herr, Craig Krampf, (Seated) Sandy Tippen

Doc Holiday and Bobby Bradley, Quad Studio

Members Of The Wailers, Doc, Bill Reid

Doc Holiday, Bobby Bradley & Mel McDaniel at Quad Studios

Doc Holiday, Garry Tallent, & The Kentucky HeadHunters At Quad Studios

Well you remember how I told you I hated that town (Nashville) and didn't like coming in there at all. I mean I even got to the point where, if I had a session at the barn, I would actually get a motel room 70 miles outside of Nashville and drive in to do the session.

I remember one night we were doing a session at the barn, and Bobby was clowning around, and I got a little pissed at him and said, "stop fuckin' around, I want to get the hell out of this damn hillbilly bullshit and get back to civilization". Just then I walked out of the barn to have a cigarette, and when I opened the door there was a herd of like six or seven fuckin' goats in the doorway. I turned around to Bobby and said, "That's fuckin' it for me, there's a bunch of God damn goats in the doorway", and Bobby looked at me and said with a big smile, "Welcome to Nashville".

Well we continued working at the barn for a couple more years and unfortunately, Owen Bradley passed away, and the barn kind of shut its doors for good. So we had to find ourselves another studio to work in. We ran into a guy called, Mark Greenwood who was the bass player for Garth Brooks. Mark was managing a studio at the time just off of Music Row in Nashville, call Quad studios. And it was for sure, a million dollar studio. The recording console alone, cost close to a million dollars. So we all agreed to give that studio a shot, and actually, I kinda like the location a little bit better than the barn, because it was more in the city of Nashville itself, and I was positive that when I went out to have a cigarette, I would not be attacked by a bunch of fucking goats.

Well after a lot of years producing and recording at Quad studios, we were getting pretty comfortable there and we did a bunch of major records and artists there. I mean a lot of major recording name artists. We did The Kentucky Headhunters there, we did Doug Kershaw, and also Bob Marley's Wailers, and Mel McDaniel just to name a few, and we were rolling pretty good. Then one day Mark came in and told us that Garth Brooks was going back on the road and going to tour again. My thoughts on that was, if Mark is leaving so are we. I mean the bottom line was, we had built a relationship up between Mark and me and my team, and like I said before, we were very comfortable there, and that made it easy for us to work and create. So needless to say we were back in the hunt for a new studio home. We had gotten an offer to go to Ronnie Milsap's studio, called the house that Ronnie built, and it was actually only a couple of blocks away from Quad. So one day when we had a break, myself, Dale and Bobby, took a walk over to check out the studio. I will say that it was a great studio, but for some reason I just didn't get the right vibe there. I really don't know why, but I wasn't feeling it, you know what I mean. So naturally we didn't take that deal, and was still looking for a new home. An offer came down the pike from Sony studios, right at the top of Music row. Once again you will remember I told you, that basically all million dollar plus studios were kind of like the same, as far as equipment was concern.

So one day, once again, me, Dale and Bobby, drove over to Sony studios. And I will say I like the place a lot right off the bat. It just had a real warm feel to it, and the good thing was they were not going to bother us in any way, but the best part was, there was no public access to the studio, so we would be in there on our own with no interference whatsoever. After I thought about it for a week or so I decided that this was the right move for us. So in short Sony studios would become the new home for Doc Holiday and his "A" team. We are now going into our sixth year at Sony, and as of the writing of this book we are still there knocking out great records. But like I always said, in this business, "Nothing Good Last Forever".

Doc Holiday And Bobby Bradley At Sony Studios, Music Row, Nashville, TN.

Jim Horn And Doc Holiday On A Break At Sony Studios

Well, I guess I kind of started ass backwards with this chapter, so it might be time to go back to the beginning of where it all started, rather than start where it all ended or is today. Going back to the mid-60s, I think the first real recording studio I was ever in or ever worked in, was a place called Mr. Music Inc., that was located in a little small town on the Jersey shore called Bricktown, it was kind of a small studio, but it was really cool just because it was an actual recording studio, and you could make records there. We used to go in there maybe three or four nights a week, and Jam, and try to write original songs and just do stuff like that, and try to learn about the whole recording scene. I guess every local musician on the New Jersey shore wound up in that studio one time or another, because in reality it was the only recording studio we even knew of. I remember one night I was there and there was this kids band from Freehold, New Jersey, cutting their first record ever. I think they were all like 14 and 15 years old, and actually were pretty good. I mean they were not great but they weren't that bad either. The name of the band was "The Castiles", they were playing a lot of local dances and shows in the area. Funny thing about that band, one of the guitar players went on to become pretty damn famous. His name was, and still is, Bruce Springsteen, and the picture below is me standing in that control room watching them record their first record. Who knew then, but in this God damn business you never know when lightning is gonna strike.

Doc Holiday In The Control Room At Mr. Music Inc., Bricktown, New Jersey, 1966

I have to make it clear that in the beginning of my career as a producer, I was pretty much centered on the East coast of the United States. Most of the studios that I worked in were located in New Jersey, Pennsylvania, New York and Massachusetts. So I guess you could say that my roots in music came from those areas, however through out my career I was able to adapt to many different kinds of music and sound. Case in point, when I move south I had no problem adapting to that style of music and delivery.

I think some of the major studios that I worked at were, the Record Plant in New York

City, Sigma Sound Studios in Philadelphia and Virtue recording studio also in Philadelphia. So you see I had a strong base for the northern R & B, Motown feel. However back in those early days there was also a strong element of a thing called Rockabilly, with the introduction of artists like, Elvis Presley, Buddy Holly and Jerry Lee Lewis. In that rockabilly vein there was a very strong element of country music, so the transformation from what I was used to in music to a more country music feel was not really that difficult.

There were other major areas that came into play that threw me for a little loop, like Miami Florida for one. There was a completely different thing going on down there, and the music was being injected by a Latin feel, that was totally obscure to me, so I had to learn that and be able to incorporate that feel, into my signature productions that was still in the development stage. So now I think you might be getting the picture. Here comes this kid from New Jersey, that had been doing Doo-Wop and Motown sounding stuff, and starting to have some serious success at doing it, is now being thrust into situations that required these other elements of music, from the different areas of the United States.

It may sound crazy to you but these little pockets/areas in the United States, all have a different sort of cultural taste, that is ever so slightly blended into the big picture that we call, rock 'n roll, country, pop or whatever label you want to put on it. The bottom line is, it's all the same bullshit. I mean let's get real here, there are only seven major notes known to mankind. How many times can you rearrange and present those same seven notes to make it sound different. Easy, you inject some of that cultural ingredients into the music, and that makes it different. Once you have figured that out, like I said, it's still the same bullshit, only now as I often say in the studio, we have dressed that whore up, by bringing in those other elements into play. For instance, if you were in Louisiana, you bring in a Cajun feel and add a little Delta blues to the stew, and there you have it. You have dressed those same 7 notes up to the point, where the basic part of the music is no longer recognizable, because of the injection of the other elements, but in reality, it's actually all the same, only now it's well hidden .

    I will admit that there are times when you have to go completely out of the box.

Like if you're doing jazz or hip-hop, then believe it or not, your creativity comes into serious play, because, even though you have all these years of experience putting together music, now you come to a type of music and sound that breaks all the rules, or what you perceive to be the rules. So in reality, you don't really change the base of the music, it is always locked in tight, in other words the basic music is the cake, you change that cake by adding different icing. How do you make it different? it's done with instruments, different sounding instruments that are blended into the basic foundation. Okay maybe now it is starting to sound a little difficult, so let me clarify it for you.

If you're doing a country record and you bring in a steel guitar, and a fiddle, it now sounds country, right? But if you take that steel guitar and fiddle out, it's no longer a country record. So it's the instruments that are associated with that type of music, that make it what it needs to be, in order to fit into that category. And it's true, not only is it the addition of different instruments, it's in the way that instrument is played, and gets you to where you need to be with that sound. I mean really folks, a fiddle is a violin, you can play it like a concert violinist, or you can play like a hillbilly fiddle player. The way it is played, that is the important part. So without a doubt, it is definitely the addition of certain instruments into the mix, but it is also the way those instruments are played that give you that recognizable sound.

Well I could go on and on with the studio stuff, but I think I made my point, or at least I hope I shed a little light on the way that I look at what I do for a living.

Doc Holiday and Garry Tallent at Quad

Doc Holiday and Becky Hobbs at Sony

The Joy of Parenthood

Throughout my life and career, I did manage to get married a few times, eight to be exact. But in those early days, I was also not a very good husband, but by far, I was the worst parent in the world. My whole early days were spent chasing that dream, of reaching the highest level I could in the entertainment business. Looking back at it now, it was a huge mistake, because when I finally reached the level I was so desperately seeking, I realized that I had sacrifice, and left a huge part of myself behind, and would never be able to get any of it back.

My first marriage took place in New Jersey. I was just performing locally, and I guess everyone around me was looking at it like it was a hobby. Little did they know at that time, it was much more than a hobby to me, it was an obsession, and I was willing to sacrifice, anything and everything to get where I wanted to be. I was dating a girl who was the head cheerleader at the local high school. Her name was Judy Dietrich, and she was totally that 50's kind of girl, right down to the sweater and the poodle skirt, plus she drove a brand-new Chevrolet Impala. So I guess you can imagine, that she was definitely eye candy at the time, and what I thought I needed to have on my arm, for that huge ego I was developing. So against the advice of everyone around me, including my parents, I wound up marrying her.

One year into that marriage, after I had purchased a three bedroom ranch, in an area known as Shadow Lake, New Jersey, which was right on the outskirts of Red Bank, my music career started to take off. I was making a lot of money, working both as a hairdresser, and performing six nights a week, so I guess you figured out by now I was hardly ever home. But when I did get home, I wanted to go out, and you know, have a classy dinner, buy expensive clothes, do all the things that the money I was making allowed me to do. Well the wife Judy, was totally against all of that. She was more of a homebody, who thought a big evening out, is going to a local restaurant, and then go home and watch television. Well as you have probably figured out by now that was not my idea of life, it should have been, but unfortunately it was not.

A little over a year into that marriage, she gave birth to my first of three children. Two children with Judy my first wife, and one child with a different Judy, who became my last wife. Yea yea, I know what you're thinking, first wife was named Judy, (and that sure as hell did not work out), and the last wife is named Judy, you would think I would see that coming, but never did.

My first child that was born, was a baby girl, and we named her Michele. I feel it necessary that you know right now, that this baby girl stole my heart. The bottom line was, if it wasn't for her, that marriage would've been over in a New York minute. I think it was at that time, I developed a behavior pattern that justified my absence, and not being there when I should have been, rather than me playing music or partying. I thought that buying Michelle every possible toy known to mankind, would suffice the void of not having that father figure around, when it should have been the other way around. To this day I am still infected with that same outlook, and in my mind the only way I can show appreciation or love is by buying and giving gifts to show my true feelings.

So like I said, my music career was starting to really take off, and the money was pouring in, but so were the distractions of the wild lifestyle, and not to mention the women, and trust me there were many of them. And the bigger I got in the entertainment industry, and the more star power I got, the farther away from reality I drifted. I look back at it now, and the reality was, I had brought a child into the world, and those moments that I miss of her growing up could never be recaptured. Her first steps, I wasn't there, her first words, I wasn't there, and the list goes on and on. For a guy that thought he was all that at the time, was in reality a fucking idiot, who gave up some of the greatest treasures, that life had to offer.

Well it got to the point of my career, that was moving so quickly, and instead of performing locally I was now on tour all over the world. My parents had moved from New Jersey to Fort Lauderdale Florida and suggested that Judy and Michelle move down there with them while I was on tour. So we sold the house in New Jersey and Judy and Michelle went to Florida to live with my parents.

One incident that I remembered that happened when they were living in Florida was, I came off the road for about a week, and went to see my baby at my mothers house, and by this time Michelle was now three years old. I remember being there for about a week, and I got a call from my agent, telling me we were booked on a tour that would last a little over a year. I recall having a conversation with my wife and telling her, I want out of this marriage, so after a little bit of an argument she agreed, it was no longer working for her or for me, and we were both two totally different people now, who wanted totally different things out of life.

The day I left on that year-long tour, Michelle came running out of the house and said, "Daddy where are you going", at that moment I had to look into the face of the only thing in the world, that was important to me, and lie. I said "I'll be right back, I'm just going to the store" and she said, "take me with you, take me with you please daddy", and once again I lied, "I'll be right back, and I'll bring you a present". I knew then that I probably would not see my baby girl for a long, long time. My mother lived on a cul de sac, so I had to drive the car to the end of the road, and turned around and pass my mother holding Michele and her arms. That image of my daughter crying with her arms out, screaming daddy take me with you, will forever be burned in my mind. I will never forget that, until they put me in the ground.

Well it was five years later that I finally got to see my daughter again. By this time she was eight years old and weeks away from her birthday turning nine years old. I was on my way back from a Canadian tour, and I arranged to stop in New Jersey at a restaurant on Highway 35 in Edison. I got in touch with Judy and asked her if she would bring the kids to meet me at the restaurant. Well the kids showed up, and in the beginning, Michelle was very withdrawn, and of course my son Eddie that I had never seen from the time he was born, had a look on his face like, who is this guy? Of course as always I was loaded down with presents for them, I mean

I spent probably $4000.00 on everything you could imagine. My son Eddie was excited. It was like Christmas in July for him, and again I really don't think he had any idea that I was his father. Michele on the other hand was far from warm, and on every answer to every question I asked her, she gave me a very subdued one word answer. I could understand the resentment from her, but that didn't make it any easier for me, there was no way I could go back in time, and change the damage. It killed me to see my daughter that way, and deep down inside, I knew that it was all my own doing.

I found out that day, that Judy had met another guy and his name was Bart. It was a scruffy looking guy, not well-dressed, and looked like something from a downtown trailer park. But hey, that was her speed, dinner at McDonald's and watching television all night. I was blown away when my son called this scumbag Dad, but I kept my cool and didn't say anything, but trust me I wanted to unload on his ass and her ass. And on top of it all he had a real fucking attitude towards me, that made me want to knock the shit out of that mother fucker, but I kept my cool.

After about an hour and a half, I gave

them all their presents, and I tried to get close with Michele on some level. I will say that she started to warm up a little, but there was an incident where this guy Bart, gave her an order in a very aggressive manner, and she spun around and said very defiantly "you're not my father". I waited patiently for him to say something back to her, and would have been all I needed to rip this mother fucker apart.

It was time to leave, and I had the whole band and crew had been in the tour bus outside waiting. As I walked to the bus Judy, Bart, and Eddie were loading the presents into their car about 30 feet away from me. Just then Michelle came running over to me as I was getting into the bus, she grabbed my arm and said, "daddy, take me with you", only this time I didn't lie, I told her I couldn't because I had another eight months to go on this tour. But I promised her that I would come back for her, and take her and her brother to Florida and take them to Disney World. And trust me folks that was the promise I was not going to break no matter what.

Sure enough I did come back in eight months, and even though there was a huge argument with their mother, and a lot of threats were thrown at her and her boyfriend Bart, I loaded up my kids on that tour bus, and we headed south on that vacation I had promise. By this time Michelle was getting ready for her 10th birthday, and she was no longer a baby. Actually she was very mature for her age, but I sensed something was not quite right, and of course I blame myself. I got them a huge penthouse suite at the Lauderdale Beach club, right on the ocean, and we did nothing but have fun 20 four hours a day. It was nothing but water parks, go-cart tracks, Disney World, you name it, if it was in the state of Florida we did it, and if it was good, we did it two and three times.

Michelle was warming up a little, there was still something strange in her behavior and I couldn't put my finger on it, so I kind of convinced myself that she was still holding some sort of a grudge against me, and my behavior as a father. So really lets face it, as a father, I sucked. Well that four week vacation turned out to be a 10 week vacation. I was turning down jobs, left and right with my agent, and on top of it I had that bitch Judy in New Jersey threatening me with calling the cops and saying that I kidnapped my kids. My response to that was "go ahead mother fucker, I will bury you and that piece of shit Bart, your fucking"

Well anyway it was time to bring the kids back, because they were already one week late in starting school. Naturally Michelle wanted no part of going back there, I mean they live in a very small apartment, a two bedroom apartment in Lawrence Harbor, New Jersey, Eddie slept in one bedroom, and Michele had the other bedroom, Judy and Bart slept on a pullout couch in the living room. There was no way I was given Judy any God damn other money, other than the monthly support for the children, which I doubted she spent on the kids in the first damn place.

When I got to New Jersey to drop the kids off, I walked into the apartment, and they were empty fucking beer cans all over the place. It was then that I found out that Bart wasn't even working, so they were living on welfare, and the money I was sending for child support. There was just something about this guy Bart that I had a bad feeling about, I mean he was the ultimate scumbag, Dirty Looking, unkempt, you know the way a fucking loser drunk looks like. But it was time for me to hit the road, and I promised

Michele that after the school year, I would come back and pick her up. But that was another promise that I could not keep, I was book for18 months and could not get back to the states in time for their summer vacation. Once again fucking music got in the way.

It would be three years until I saw my kids again, that was quite by accident. I was performing at a place called the Executive Inn, in Evansville, Indiana opening for the group the Fifth Dimension. We had just started the tour and were only two weeks into it. I was in my hotel room and got a call from the front desk, telling me that my daughter was in the lobby. I figured it was just some fan pulling a scam to try to get to my room. I told the front desk, no way, my daughter is only 13 years old. And he responded "that's how old she looks Doc".

So I got dressed and went down to the lobby, and sure enough, there was Michelle. She had taken a bus, at only 13 years of age remember, rode the bus by herself, to Newark Airport, bought a ticket with money that she stole from her mother, to Evansville Indiana, by herself, and flew to where I was at, after she talked to my mother, and my mom told her where I was at. All by herself, not telling anyone what she was planning to do. She had called my mother in Florida, and asked her where I was at, because she wanted to talk to me. But instead at 13 years old, she got on that damn plane and flew out. It was then and only then, that I found out what was going on in that apartment.

Well, this is the story in a nutshell. It seems that two nights before Michele arrived in Indiana, her mother and then boyfriend Bart, got seriously drunk at home. Her brother Eddie was spending the night doing a sleep over at a friends house, and Michele's mother had passed out on her couch in a drunken stupor. It was then that her drunk ass boyfriend entered my daughters room, and began fondling her while she was asleep. Michele woke up, only to find him on top of her attempting to rape her. Naturally she screamed for her mother, but again her mother was drunk on her ass and passed out.

After hearing her story, needless to say I went fuckin' berserk. The first thing I did was take my daughter to an emergency room to see if she had been, sexually assaulted within the last 48 hours. Well the tests came back positive, the 13-year-old had been assaulted, and the doctors said it was a violent assault, leaving bruises and marks all over her private area.

I have to admit my first thought was to go there and kill this fucking bastard. Now remember I am on tour with the Fifth Dimension, so the way I handled it, and it might have been the wrong way looking back at it now, was to make plans to leave the tour and fly back to New Jersey, leaving Michele in Indiana with my present wife. Like I said looking back at it, that may not have been the right thing to do, I should have involved the cops in some way, but chose to deal with it in my own way, The Jersey street way.

I got to New Jersey by flying into Newark airport 48 hours later. I had phoned ahead for two friends that I had known from Jersey, who some may not think were very nice people, however they were the kind of people I needed for what I wanted to do.

After landing in Jersey, my two friends were there to meet me, and we headed towards Lawrence Harbor where Judy and her boyfriend lived. I will admit now that this was going to be a very short meeting. There were going to be no questions asked, or discussions taken place. The bottom line was he was going to die. There would be no court case, there would be no publicity, for what had happened to my daughter, but I guarantee you, there would be one dead body, and if she got in the way there would be two. To put it simply, this would be my justice.

Well we arrived at the apartment, and the three of us got out of the car, and Frankie said to me, "let us handle this, you stay in the car, this will be clean and quick". I said to Frankie, "no I want to see the bastard". So anyway I guess they realized there was no talking me out of it, so we headed to the front door. I knocked on the front door with Frankie in Sal on my left and right, and was shocked when someone opened the door, and they were like 20 people in the apartment. Sal pushed me away, and Frankie said to me, "which one is the mother fucker we want?. I didn't even get a chance to answer, because of the commotion that was going on in that apartment. It seemed that Bart had died six hours earlier from a massive heart attack, and all the people there were comforting Judy. Karma, I guess is a bitch, but the worst thing was, I didn't get to see the son of a bitch die. Well it did not end there, I mean really did you think I would just going to walk away, I figured there was still a score to settle with my ex-wife, so we push our way into the apartment and I approached her with fire in my eyes.

If you thought there was commotion going on grieving over the loss of that piece of shit, the best was yet to come. With Frankie and Sal at my side, I walked right up to her and told her what I was there for, and I didn't say it in a quiet voice, everyone in that room heard me. Needless to say there was a lot of confusion, and one of her friends husband grab my arm, and was screaming for me to get out. Just then Frankie, hit this guy a shot to the head that knocked him flat on his ass. Okay, now it's getting crazy. Just then Sal grabbed me and said "let's get the fuck out of here now, some bitch is calling the cops". So Frankie and Sal rushed me out of there and we jumped in the car and headed back to Newark.

On the way back, I was still foaming at the mouth, I didn't get to do what I wanted to do, and there was no closure for me at all. I remember Frankie telling me, "relax, we will handle this, you get on the plane and get the hell out of here, I promise you we will handle this". So now all I am left with is to attempt to handle it in a legal manner, which would be difficult because the cock sucker was dead.

Needless to say by this time there was a lot of turmoil in my life, my daughter's life, and my family's life. It lasted for many years, and my ex-wife denied it ever happened. The bottom line was I know, it did happen, and more importantly so did my daughter.

From that point on my daughter Michele lived a life of torment, she never really ever got over it, and it affected her, every day of the rest of her life.

When Michele turned 29 years old, she was a passenger in a car accident. It seemed the person driving the car, hit a brick wall at 60 miles an hour. Michele was in the passenger seat and not wearing a seat belt, and her whole body was thrown through the windshield, and she hit a brick wall with her body. Because of the injuries she sustained from that accident, it was very difficult for her to stand or walk in a normal manner, and the constant pain she was in was unbearable. There was nothing that could be done medically to correct her injuries, so it was then that the doctors prescribed pain medication, so she could deal with everyday life in somewhat of a normal manner.

As the years went by, Michele became more dependent on the pain medication, just to get through the day. I tried for years to get her off of that dependency, but in short she was addicted, and although she and I made many attempts to stop her addiction, she would never be successful at it. The strange thing about it all was, I never realized how much pain that kid of mine was in, until I myself was stricken with the same medical problems later in life

My current wife Judy had become very close to Michele, ever since that incident in Indiana. Michele was living in New Jersey, and we were living in Virginia, but my wife spoke to her at least four times a week on the phone, and they were not short conversations, they lasted some times two and three hours.

Then one night I was in my room and I glanced over at the phone extension in my room, and noticed that it said line in use. I picked up the phone and it was my wife talking to Michele. It was 1 AM in the morning, and I remember telling Michele, "you have to get off of that shit, I will help you". She said "Dad, I have to be medically detox before I can go to rehab, if I just go to rehab, it will throw my body into shock, and it will kill me". I said "no problem, you come here and I'll have one of my doctor friends, get you into the hospital and clean you out". Well after about 15 minutes, she agreed to do it, and I said I would make the plane reservations. This was on a Sunday night, and she told me she wanted to leave Tuesday morning because she had a lawyer's appointment Monday afternoon, where she was finally getting a settlement check for $30,000 for that accident. I told her all right, I'll get the ticket and you leave Tuesday morning. We stayed on the phone with her until around 1:30 in the morning and I got on the computer and booked her flight. It was then that I received the worst phone call any parent could receive. It was now 3 AM in the morning, and my nephew Tommy was on the phone. He told me Michele had died in her apartment, they found her dead on the floor. So at the young age of 44 my baby was gone. This was the hardest chapter I had to write in this book and, I hope no parent reading this will never have to write one like it.

Michele (Age 35)

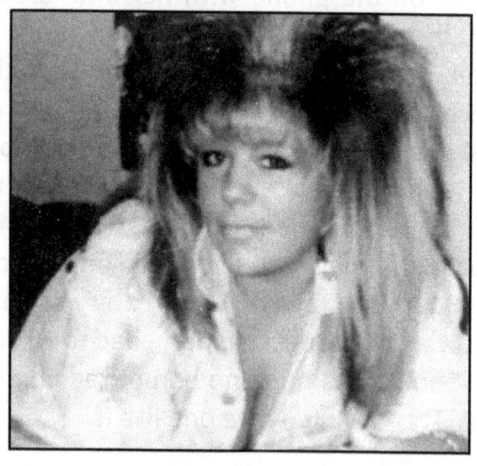

Michele (Age 25)

Then came a ray of sunshine for me, the birth of my daughter Carmela, and I was determined to do this one different. There was no way that fucking music business was gonna get in the way of raising this child.

I remember when the subject first came up about having a baby between myself and my current wife, and ironically still my wife at the time of the writing of this book, who by the way was and is 12 years younger than me. I said to her, "do you really want to take on the responsibility of raising a child"? Her answer was quick and easy "It's what I have wanted since grade nine". I mean really, I was getting old at the time and started to wear out a little, and to be honest with you, that marriage with her, in my opinion was not the best thing that happen in my life at that point. But it was OK. She was very self centered and because of her height (Just under 5 ft.) she had a huge Neapolitan complex. But really in the end that marriage turned out pretty damn good, actually really fuckin' good. My health started to fail, and my wife became a tremendous caretaker for me and in time became my whole world. So all those things that happened in my past, I was able to somewhat put in the pass, and live more into today. I mean really folks, what's done is done, you can't change the past, but you sure as hell can make the present better, by letting go of the bull shit of yesterday.

So anyway when we found out that my wife was pregnant, I was in a place called Hampton Virginia, bailing out a nightclub that I had invested in, that was about $2 million in debt. It took me approximately six months to get the place out of debt to where it was once again making money.

In the meantime my wife had been going to see a doctor, because she was pregnant of course. The doctors name was John Lockhart, and his reputation around that area, was that he was the best when it came to delivering babies. Plus my wife felt secure with him, and this being her first child, and only child I might add, that security with your doctor carried a lot of weight,

It also seemed that this doctor had found out who I was, and that I was in the music business, and a pretty hot record producer at the time. So here's where I found out, that this doctor was also a songwriter, and every time my wife would come back from her doctors visits, she mentioned that he had asked her to mention to me, that he had a strong desire to record a song he had written for his mother that had passed away from Cancer. Naturally I shrugged it off every time, and told her I wasn't interested, but that never stopped her from mentioning it every damn time she went to the doctors office.

Like I said I had gotten the club out of debt, sold my interest in it and made a pretty good profit, and I felt it was time for us to head back to Miami. Well, she was having no part of that, she said she wasn't going anywhere until that baby was born. So I had no choice in the matter but to stick around Virginia, so she could stay with this doctor until the baby was born.

Now you have to remember with my other kids, I was never around to go thru the pregnancy thing, nor was I there when they were born. I was out there touring, playing music, and to be honest with you, when my son was born it was like four months after wards that I actually found out about him. But like I said in the beginning of this segment I was going to do things different this time with this child, so I stuck around and went through all the steps. But once again, every time she came back from the doctor's office, she tried to pressure me into listening to this guy's song, and once again I blew it off.

Well, it should be noted at this time, that my wife is very short, actually she's like 5 foot tall, and this was a very rough pregnancy for her, she gained like 70 pounds. She weighed around the hundred pounds before she got pregnant and blew up to 170 pounds. Of course nothing runs smooth, and the baby was one week late, and her doctor informed her that he was going to do a cesarean birth, and it would take place at Wednesday at 8 AM.

So for the first time in my life I decided to go with her into the operating room, and see the birth of my daughter. Now get this, that doctor is operating on her, cutting into her stomach, and while he is doing that, he's pitching me the song he wanted to record. OK, well right now I'm shitting in my pants, and I looked down at her stomach that had just been caught wide open, and I'm not ashamed to admit it, I started to pass out, and I remember the doctor saying to a nurse that was standing alongside of me, who was like 5 foot three, Yelling "catch him, catch him" meaning for her to grab me before I hit the floor. I mean you gotta be kidding me,

I'm 290 pounds, and this nurse that was supposed to be catching me, probably weighed 120 pounds soaking wet.

Well anyway I kept it together and didn't pass out, but I did say to him, "look just do what you're supposed to be doing there and I promise you I will listen to your song when you're done".

Well long story short, Carmela is born and I am the proud father of a baby girl.

My wife Judy and daughter Carmela

I remember telling my wife the next day, that now we had both made the decision, to bring a child into the world, there was a few things that I needed to happen in order to be comfortable. Number one was I would never allow my child to be spanked, ever!, And the second thing I needed was to move out of the states and moved to our house on the island in Canada, and for the first couple of years, raise her on the island, versus in Miami where we were currently living. Yeah I know I told you I got my house in Virginia but that was just until she had the baby, I still had my house in Miami.

So she agreed with me and we loaded up and moved to the island of Caribou, Canada. At first it was really different, it was quiet, there was no hustle and bustle whatsoever, but we had a great house in a great location and we were right on the water, I mean you could walk 100 feet outside my back door and there was the beach. So even though it was a big change from Miami, it was a good change. It was me, my wife and Carmela, living on the beach, that we owned, and no interference from any neighbors what so ever.

The House On Caribou Island

The View From The Back Deck

All that lasted for about six months, and I started to get the urge for the music business again. So I built myself a studio on that island. At first it was just for my own personal use, but before you know it I'm looking for artist to record, only problem was, we were living on an island in the middle of the ocean, and on this island there was probably only four families living on it, which meant I had to go on the mainland to see any talent that was available. But in the meantime I was having fun raising Carmela.

Well a year or so went by and here we were, the happy family on the island, I had my recording studio, and I found a few acts on the mainland that I was working with, so everything is really cool, or at least I thought it was.

You have to remember I am in Canada on an island, and I am not a Canadian citizen, which means I am not supposed to be working there and earning money, but I'm getting away with it because again we were isolated on that island.

Carmela is now approximately a year and a half old, and she isn't speaking correctly, she still doing baby talk and not pronouncing words. So I said to my wife one day,

Carmela In The Home Studio On The Island

something is wrong with her, because the kid should be speaking at a year and a half. Well, my mother came up from Florida to visit, and I voice my concerns to her about Carmela not speaking. My mother spent about two days with her and came to me one day and said, "she's talking, she's talking good". I told her, I thought she was crazy because you couldn't understand anything Carmela was saying. Just then my mother said to me she is speaking, fluent French, and that's when we figured it all out.

Seems that Carmela was watching the television show call, Sesame Street, however it was being broadcast from Quebec, and it was being broadcast in French. Terrific, my kid is speaking French and I don't understand a word of French. So right then I started to think, hey maybe it's time to get back to civilization. Plus the fact that there were no kids on that island other than Carmela, so she really wasn't getting any interaction with other kids. I mean her friends were a big rock garden in the back, and in the house we had ceiling to floor mirrors and she would stand in front of the mirror is and talk to her reflection.

Well, I had almost made up my mind that we were going to leave, and just then we get a notice from manpower and immigration in Canada, that informed me that I had, 30 days to leave the country because I was working without landed immigrant status or a working visa. So now it is final, we are getting the hell off the island and back to civilization.

Here we are leaving, Canada and on my way to Miami, only this time I had a baby girl, oh I forgot, and a great wife. Well the move from the island would not be an easy one. You see I had accumulated three automobiles, a ton of studio equipment, and a complete house full of furniture, and I had drawn out of the bank $160,000.00 in cash that I had at the time in Canada. I guess you could tell by now, I had no intentions of coming back. I was so set on getting the hell off of that island, I probably made one of the biggest mistakes in my life. I called one of our neighbors on the island, who had become a very close friend of me and my family. He was a lobster fisherman, and three or four times a week, he would bring by anywhere between 10 and 20 cooked lobsters. You see in order to ship lobster from Canada to the United States, they had to be a minimum of 1 pound, so any one of them that weighed less than that, they would cook up on the pier, and he would bring them by and give them to us. His name was Don, and like I said, he became a good friend. Once I had decided that I was leaving and never returning, I gave Don a call. You see Don always loved our house, because we were right on the water. I was impatient to get out of there, I will admit that, any way, when I called Don, I said, "Don, I'm leaving the island, and I know you like my house, so I'm going to my attorneys office tomorrow, and I'm going to have her draw up papers, and give you the house". Don replied, "Doc, I can't afford to buy that house and property". I said, "Not a problem Don, I'm giving it to you for free". And that's what I did, and looking back at it now, it would probably the biggest mistake that I made in my life. I should have kept it, but it is what it is and I did what I did. So I called in three friends from the states to help me move all of that shit. I had Brian Parker who was from Hampton Virginia, drive one of the cars, and another guy called Luke Wallace, who was also from Hampton Virginia, drive the other car. I rented a huge truck to move all the equipment and furniture, and I called my old roadie Blake to fly up and drive the truck.

It was a long ass drive and I remember we stopped in a motel in Massachusetts, to get a night sleep before we headed back out. That cash I had told you about, was in an attache case, and believe it or not, I had it handcuffed to Blake, and to this day he never knew what was in that case.

So we hit Virginia, and my plan was to sell two of the cars in Virginia, and then have Blake drive the truck to Miami. Well as always nothing seem to go as planned. The reason I stopped in Virginia was because Luke and Brian live there, and the second reason was I intended to take that cash and turn it into a certified check or something like that. Well four days went by in Virginia, and Blake informed me that after he dropped the truck off in Miami, he was coming back to Hampton Virginia and set up a business. So after a lot of thinking and soul-searching, I decided what the hell, lets stay in Virginia for a while, I mean my wife like it there, I had a lot of friends there, and it was really a good place at the time to raise Carmela. So I rented a big four-bedroom ranch house on a place called Lilac court. There was only three houses on the court, so I had my privacy, and the best was in that neighborhood there were kids around the same age as Carmela.

I had no intentions of working for the next couple of years, and really just wanted to concentrate on having fun with my daughter. And I promise you that I did. I spent a lot of time with her.

The funny thing was she had her days and nights mixed up. She would sleep in the daytime and be up to four or 5 AM in the morning. I can remember laying in bed and she would run into the room, stand at the foot of the bed and say, "daddy announced me". I would say "ladies and gentlemen, just returning from her record-breaking tour, before the crown heads of Europe, please give a warm welcome, to Carmela", and she would go into this crazy dance, singing at the top of her lungs for like five minutes straight. And this took place almost every night, and it wasn't just one time a night, she would keep doing it and doing it until she was completely exhausted and went to sleep.

Carmela Performing at 3am.

At the time we had a big chow chow dog, she weighed about 80 pounds, and look like a lion. Carmela named her Beatrice, and those two were inseparable. I mean it even got to the point, where Beatrice would actually sleep with her in her bed.

Carmela And Beatrice, Ready To Sleep?

Carmela And Beatrice Best Of Friends

Well looking back at it now, life was good, but as you expected, I couldn't stay away from that damn music too long, so just for kicks I set up a small studio in the house, you know just to fool around for my own personal use. I think it was during that time that I finally realize, I was addicted to the music, and before you know it I was up to my neck in it again.

I had gotten real friendly with a couple name, Fonda and Tom Breeden and they owned a very small recording studio in Hampton Virginia, and like I said before you know it, I was in there producing records 5 to 6 days a week.

Carmela was getting older now and it was almost time for her to start school. So we looked around for a house to buy, and we found one in the James River section of Newport News, Virginia. It was a huge house, it had five bedrooms, a big ass den, and a huge Florida room in the rear of the house, plus it had a large fenced in yard, so Beatrice could run free.

We bought the house, put in a swimming pool, and enrolled Carmela into a private school called Montessori.

Now you have to remember that basically I am a road dog, I mean I spent my whole life on tour, so it was questionable how long I could stay in one place. But it was different this time around I had responsibilities. Those days of just packing up and moving all around the world, for all intensive purposes were over. So, I guess you can imagine it was only a matter of time before I was up to my neck in the music business again.

I began traveling a lot to different studios all over the United States, but I spent a lot of time at home. My success had created a huge income, and I really didn't have to work that much, so all in all I got to spend a lot of time with Carmela.

You know it's ironic, that all my kids inherited my musical talents, but none of them wanted to go into the music business. But that was okay, I mean that business had taken the best years of my life, and continued to do so, and trust me it wasn't easy.

Well Carmela grew up to be my pride and joy, and most of the time I respected her decision on life's matters. She grew up into a very creative person, which may be in some peoples eyes, thought that she was a little strange, in the way she dressed or handled herself in different situations. But hey I can't fault her for that, she was who she was, and most of all, she was basically happy, with who and what she had become.

I will tell you that she wanted for nothing, she always got the best of the best, sports cars, clothes, you name it, she always had the best that money could buy. A funny thing about that was, she never asked for anything. She would be speaking about a certain subject, and the next thing you know, what ever I thought she desired, I made it happen. Once again I guess it was my way of saying I love you.

I always used to refer to my daughter Michele, as the one who keeps me up at night, worrying that is. Will now that Michele is gone, I will admit that Carmela has taken over that role. There were occasions when she accompanied me on business trips, and I look forward to them, and treasure them to this day.

While Michele was alive, I got to spend a few trips with the two of them together, and that my friends will be the greatest memory I will ever have.

There was no denying that both of them were my daughter's, there was no DNA test needed on either of them, they looked like me, they talked like me, and they sure as hell acted like me. But that was okay, because I think, ME, ain't so god damn bad after all. As a matter of fact, she cost me more living on her own, then she did when she was living at home, but once again I love being able to do it for her, and wouldn't have it any other way.

Today Carmela has moved out, and is on her own, and I guess she feels pretty proud of that. However truth be known, I still pay her car payment, her car insurance, her cell phone bill, and a part of her rent, but that's okay I'm glad to do it, and the celebrity moonshine business, which is extremely lucrative, I put that company in her name 100%, and each month she gets a very hefty check from that business.

So today as of the writing of this book, Carmela is 29 years old. She got my brains and my drive for success, and got her mother's attitude. But that's okay too, I wouldn't trade it for the world. So like I said earlier in this chapter, I was going to raise this child different, I was going to be there 110%, and I think I accomplished that.

I hope my wife and child realizes my dedication, to the both of them, I really doubt it, once again because of the problem I have always had in showing my love But at lease I could sleep at night knowing, I was there for it all, They both came first, and if they don't realize it they sure as hell will after I am gone.

My two Daughters Carmela and Michele

Carmela and Me At The Grammy Awards

Carmela On Her Way to a Comic Con

Carmela age 26

Judy and Carmela Age 3

Carmela, always an Animal Lover

The Nashville Hustle, The Hillbilly Con Train

Well I discovered one thing. The farther I got into the music industry in Nashville, the more I realized how corrupt, crooked, and what a con game it was. Now, I'm not talking about the major artist. I'm talking about the vanity labels, and independent recording artists. There are hundreds of them out there pouring into Nashville everyday. An endless stream of wannabe stars. The different, little small record labels that offer services to young stars who are coming to Nashville and want to record in Nashville and make it to the "Big Time". And these Gooberville con men usually bring them into these small bull shit computer driven studios with the same session players making the rounds in the "Music City". They're all cookie cutters? They just knock the stuff out sounding all the same. It's not major label quality, not even close, but in their brain these vanity labels are doing to the artist what the artist thinks, " Hey, I'm a big recording star in Nashville!"

To prove that point, they create these make believe radio/record charts that have you at number 2, and Waylon Jennings is at number 4. Or, you're at number 3, and Johnny Cash is at number 6. And you think," Hey, I'm beating Johnny Cash!" "I'm beating Waylon Jennings," In realty, your not beating anybody! It's a fake chart it's all bullshit! It has no bearing what so ever on the reality of what is really happening! It's created and done just to take the artists money. And most of these vanity labels/studios have a flat fee for their so called services. One song for $1200.00, and we'll promote it for $2000.00, (actually they are all different fees, BUT it's still the same bullshit). And once you have recorded and what they called "Released" you get to ride the "HILLBILLY CON TRAIN" you'll get these fake chart numbers and a few radio reports from radio stations that have a listening audience of like 10 people in the middle of Butt Fuck North Dakota . At the end of the day, you think you're a big star, and you go down to the corner mention your name to somebody, and nobody knows who the fuck you are! I personally look at these charts sometimes, and I see all these artists names, and I say, " Who the hell are these fuckin' people?" Where do they come from? And it goes on and on and on and it was like that in Nashville 40 years ago and it's still like that now today. These vanity labels are still doing the same bullshit over and over and getting away with it.

I'll tell you a true story. I recorded an artist called Richie Balin. He was a phenomenal artist and still performing today. We went out, and we popped the first record on him, and it made it to Billboard. It reached like number 50 on Billboard, which by the way is a solid legitimate chart. The artist, (Richie) was really great and deserved to be there and maybe even higher on that chart. The second record on him came out was number 45 on Billboard, so he's on the move in the industry and he's touring performing live dates to big crowds, A big Plus factor. The Third record was released, and there was a promo team in Nashville, that was headed by a guy known as Chuck D that we decided to do the promotion on this release.

So in short Chuck wound up as one of the promo teams on the Richie Balin third release. The Billboard promo was not done by Chuck, it was done by a guy name Gene Kennedy. Gene Kennedy was legit across the board and delivered all he said he would. Chuck, we later found out, was nothing but a god damn con man and a thief. He called me in and he said, " Listen, I just debuted him at number 80 on this chart that was Cashbox." Not Billboard, but Cashbox "Can I get a bonus for bringing him in so high". And I'm sitting in his office and I said," Ah 80 debut." "That's pretty damn good ya know!" " This is his third record, and he debuts at 80." And while I'm talking to him, I look on the floor in the corner of his office and there's a stack of 45 records there. I reach down and I picked up one of the records, and it's Richie's record! It hasn't even been shipped to radio! No Cashbox radio stations had it what so ever, but yet they're showing it at number 80 on the charts with these fake radio stations supposedly playing it. At that point I said, "This is a bunch of horseshit!, and you want a fuckin bonus???"

Now with the Cashbox charts, they (Chuck D. and his crew), are controlling the back 50. So, in other words, any place in from number 50 to 100 on the charts they can put the records wherever they want, even though they're not getting played any place. Now here is the greatest unspoken con ever in "Music City". Up pops a new organization called SESAC. There was BMI, and there was ASCAP, and there was also now SESAC. These were all primary publishing and songwriter organization/unions that are use to make sure the songwriters and publishers get paid when somebody uses their music. But In order for SESAC to make it's headway into the publishing game, they said, " We are not gonna scan or pay according to actual radio plays or sales." " We are not gonna pay by radio plays." "We're not gonna scan radio stations." " We're gonna pay for chart position." "If the record gets into the 90's, we'll pay $3,000.00 to the writers and publishers." "If it get's into the 80's, we'll pay another $3,000.00." "Into the 70's, we'll pay another $3,000.00." "into the 60's, we'll pay another

3,000.00." So do the math, that's 12 grand if your record is in the 50's. Unbeknownst to SESAC, these Nashville promotion guys are totally controlling the back 50! From 50 to 100, and I might add all under the watchful eye of the publisher and owner of Cashbox, George, they're putting records wherever and whenever they wanted. So what they do is they take a record, and they'll go to Cashbox and they'll say, " Ok, we need this record at # 92. The guy will say, " I need some radio reports." They'll do what they call paper ads. There is no radio station actually playing it, there is no spins, there is no plays. Paper ads are all fake reports most of them filled out by the program directors or DJ's on these small stations who were usually on the take from these Promo guys, (NOT ALL OF THEM BUT MOST). They'll bring the records in at number 90, grab $3,000.00 from SESAC, and next week they'll move it to number 82, grab another 3 grand. The next week they'll move it into the 70's. Grab another 3. Next week, move it into the 60's and grab another week and the next week it will drop out of the charts. It's gone. It's history. It's up, and then out. I mean, it doesn't even like creep it's way down. It just goes out of the charts.

And, ya know ya say, "12 grand, well that ain't a lot of money." They're working 10 records a week. They're making $90,000.00 a week off of SESAC ALONE!!!! just by manipulating the charts.

Well, low and behold Cashbox hires a new guy to do their charts. His name is Kevin Hughes. Kevin Hughes is a young kid, Sharp kid. He sees that the charts are being manipulated by Chuck D. and his crew and He makes an announcement to Chuck D., "Listen, this fuckin' bullshit ain't gonna keep going on." "I need to have legitimate radio charts." "Otherwise, I'm not gonna do this number game you guys are pullin'." We'll they argued with him, and of course you're taking a lot of money from these guys, but Kevin stuck to his guns. He said, "I'm not gonna do it." "Either they are legitimate radio charts, or I'm not gonna do it." Sadly, a week later, Kevin Hughes was shot on Music Row at broad daylight. No one was ever brought to trial on it or convicted of the crime.

Now I can't prove it, but I'm telling you right now it was because of those charts. You hit somebody for $90,000.00 a week, your life is worthless when it comes to this kind of organized crime. Especially when you're dealing with scum like that.

Now they are in trouble at Cashbox. The heat is really on them. They can't chart their records, and SESAC gets smart. They said, " Ok, we're not doing this bullshit anymore." " We're gonna start scanning radio plays and sales" so now that little hustle they had going is gone or at lease for the SESAC side of it. BUT, they still have these young artists all coming to Nashville to be big superstars. So, they need a chart that they can control. And there's a magazine in Texas called, The Indie Bullet ran by a guy called Roy Hause, Jason H., and Gary B. is the promo man for the magazine. This chart is total bullshit! There is no legitimacy to the chart at all, but they would take a guy, Joe Blow, record him in Nashville, charge him $3,500.00 to record, they would release the record (or what they call "release"), charge him another $2,500.00 to promote it, and low and behold he would show up on that worthless chart on Indie Bullet. The artist would think, " Oh man!" " I'm climbing the charts" " I'm gonna be a big star!" No ya not man ! They are conning your ass! They are ripping you off! And to prove my point all you had to do was check your BMI or ASCAP royalties to see what you earned from radio air play and you would have seen 15 cents if you were lucky, most artists never saw one cent, but by the time the artists figured that all out, it was too late, they already got the "Nashville Hustle". And you might say, "OK, that was then, things are different now." I got news for you, they are still doing it today ! The same labels (Different names), the same people are still in it today ripping off artist left and right. The Horror stories coming out of Nashville are unbelievable.

Anyway, Chuck D. and the Nashville crew could not completely control the Texas crew of the Indie Bullet Magazine or Cashbox magazine and they needed a chart to keep the con game going, so they created this magazine called, " Indie Tracker." Indie Tracker is run by a girl, Audrey, who is dating Chuck D. and I might add is controlled by Chuck and his crew. They do the same thing. Phony charts. The whole nine yards. They even go as far as having an, Indie Tracker Award show in Nashville at some shit hole Nashville bar/club. These artist travel in for the award show from all over the globe, thinking it's like a big deal, BUT here's the deal they are gonna give the award to whatever artist has the most financial backing that they know is gonna come with 3 or 4 record releases and they got a controlled chart so they are making the call and it's total bullshit. It's unbelievable. All smoke and mirrors.

Sooner or later Indie Tracker and Indie Bullet start fighting Gangland style. There's a serious feud going on. Now ya got Texas fighting these heavy hitters (Mobsters for a better word) in Nashville. You know whose gonna win that fight right?. Next thing you know, Indie Bullet goes out of business. And Roy H disappears. I mean it got to the point where they actually sent a dead fish to Roy H in the mail. It was organized crime at it's highest level. Well, before ya know it, Indie Bullet is out. Gone completely, Roy H becomes M.I.A. and never heard from again and low and behold, Gary B. moves to Nashville and he joins the Chuck D. crew. And now the con is really on. They've got all the artists from both magazines, they got the Indie Tracker magazine (That they own), they got the charts and they're making money hand over fists. But, always remember, it's all bullshit! It's called vanity labels and fake charts. They do it for the vanity of the artist. And I don't care who you talk to, you will never see one major star that came off of one of those vanity labels charting in one of those fake ass charts. It's just totally unbelievable that they get away with it, and they are still doing it today.

You look at some of these make believe charts today, they can't do it too much in the USA so they are pumping them over in Europe. And they are going to Australia and these small community radio stations that have no power, no clout whatsoever AND they now have internet stations to get reports from. I mean really who the hell listens to internet radio, give me a break!!!. The reality of it all, if you want to be the next Garth you need those 50,000 and up watt stations The artist is not making any money on internet stations, and they have these playlist and ya see some of these DJ's (not all of em' now, just some of em' a few of these internet stations are totally legit), but some of these European stations put up their playlist that they have in their show on the internet weekly, and it shows 250 records being played in a show. And today, ya got more phony charts all over the place. One is this girl named Joyce. This is a joke! 200 records on her chart. OK, and of the 200 of em', 50 of the people on that chart are dead! They're fuckin' dead! They're not even recording. They're not even active in the business! It's hilarious, but it keeps going on. And, it goes on today. And that my friend is the Nashville horror story! They are cookie cutter labels, they take your money, they give you fake charts, they give you fake information, and you're broke, and at the end you're right back where you started from but now your a broke ass artist with no place to go. Welcome to the Nashville hustle

Back Room Deals, Smoke And Mirrors

Back room deals, you heard that right, back room deals. More goes on behind the scenes in the record industry and music industry, then the public is ever aware of. Sometimes, even the artist don't have a clue, to what takes place behind closed doors. That my friends, most of the time, is where the manipulation or what they like to call it takes place. Deals on what direction is going to be taken, with the artist or the record. Those closed-door sessions are where the make it or break it deals take place on 99%, of every hit artist or record to hear on the radio, and like I said, the public is totally blind and kept away from those facts.

Radio airplay. Really folks, how the hell do you think radio, number one, even gets the damn record to begin with. And after they get to record, what makes them want to play it. On an average week, there are 200+ new records released to the public, radio, and retail. The people in the know figure that 2 of those records released that week, will make it to the top 100 on the Billboard charts.

Looking at it this way, do you honestly think that a program director, at a radio station, has the time to listen to each and every record released, and pick out the ones that are going to be the next big hit?

For the lack of a better term, it called promotion, but in reality, it's plain and simple payola. That's right you heard me, only now its not called payola anymore, it's called, promotional gratuity, and whoever has the most money, and the biggest machinery behind them, survives in today's marketplace.

I'm sure some of you have listen to your radio, and heard some of the biggest piece of shit songs and artist, being played, constantly. How can that be? It's like I just got through telling you, it's a bought and sold product, and you the public are the ones that are being scammed and lead like a herd of sheep.

I personally have been involved in a lot of backroom deals in my career, one in particular, was at a major record label office in New York City. And at that meeting, or how they all like to call a meeting. A strategic layout on the path of the artist and the record would be layed out. A top executive at that label, said to convince everyone else in the room, and I quote, "with enough money behind it, I could get a fart to the number one position on the Billboard charts.

So you see, it's not really about how the record sounds, or what the artist sounds like, it's about the promo men, and label executives, on what they figure, they can get over on the public with. And more importantly, what they can get longevity out of. By that I mean, how long can they keep that artist and that sound, in a selling position. That's why you see, most artists today are young, because youth automatically gives them longevity.

And you also notice that a big percentage of artists today, are extremely good-looking. The cosmetic value of an artist appearance, holds more weight than their ability to sing or perform. Stage performance, (singing and performing), hell that can all be manufactured and taught.

I mean really folks, Just give a moment of thought to this. If me and you were executives at a major record label, and a kid named Bob Dylan walked in the office, and started to sing, how long do you think it would take either one of us, to get out of our chairs, and say, "are you fucking kidding me"?

I remember an incident that happened quite a number of years ago in New York City. Back in the day. Now if you had a band, it was mandatory that you got a band photo taken, you know, a promo shot of the group, and there were a number of photographers in New York City that specialize in band pictures.

Well you remember I told you about how the industry is so cosmetic today, you know what you look like versus, if you even sound good. Well that is not a new thing at all, it's been like that for many, many years. Case in point, the singer Fabian, great looking guy, couldn't sing a fucking note, but that didn't stop him from becoming one of the hottest singers in that era, proving once again that looks and appearance outweighed the talent almost every single time. Don't get me wrong, there were some awesome entertainers throughout the history of the music business, but every once in a while one of those back room deals got together, and created a minimal talent into a superstar.

There was an agent in Pennsylvania, that specialize in bullshit acts. His name was Gabe Garland, and this guy would book bands all over the country, using famous names of different bands, not the real bands, just their names. Only problem was, when the band showed up, none of the players or performers were the actual original members. So what he was doing was taking a band like, the Box Tops, who had a number one record in the 60s, and he would put a band together and call them the Box Tops. That was happening all over the country. At one time there were eight different acts out there calling themselves, the Platters, and six different acts calling themselves, the Drifters. All phony acts, but most of the public were never aware of the scam. These phony acts would actually learn all the hits of the groups, they were pretending to be, and the public ate it up thinking they were the real deal.

So getting back to this agent in

Pennsylvania. There was an incident, where he actually took four guys that were mechanics, at a local Pontiac dealership, dress them up in matching outfits, and took a high end band photograph of them. Now remember, these guys did not play any instruments or sang whatsoever, they were mechanics in a car dealership, but looking at the picture, they were four good-looking guys that looked like a band.

Wait, it gets better. So he sends this picture out to different nightclubs around the country, remember now, no one has heard this band perform, they just see a good-looking picture of four good-looking guys that look like a band. Here's the topper, he actually booked a tour for this band in 16 nightclubs across the United States.

Now here's the deal. He's got 16 weeks booked on a band, that is not a band, booked once again just off the appearance.

So he actually puts a real band of musicians together, none of which were in that picture, however to make it work, and he talks two of the mechanics in the picture, to quit their jobs, offering them more money then they are getting on their job, and joined the band that he had put together. So now legally he does have two members from that picture, however remember, that they didn't play an instrument, so he actually paid them to stand on the stage, one played a tambourine, and the other played a cowbell.

So you see, that cosmetics and appearances to sell an artist is not a new thing. So when you see one of these hot young artists today that looks so great, remember, are you buying the talent and the music, or are you once again buying the smoke and the mirrors created by another backroom deal.

This is a true story. I'm booked in a place called the Holiday Inn in Greenville, South Carolina, and it was about a 4 to 500 seat show room. The club was owned by a guy called Bob Greene, and it was by far the hottest club in Greenville,

We are booked into the club for six days, and I was doing two shows a night. On Thursday of that week we picked up the local newspaper, because they were doing a story on me performing at that club that week. While I was thumbing through the newspaper, I noticed an ad for Friday night at another club in town. They were advertising the New Century Platters, by the way, was a totally bogus group. Now here's the strange thing, right next to that ad is an another ad, from a totally different club in town, advertising the appearance of Tony Williams and the Platters.

For those of you who do not know who Tony Williams is, this is the voice, this was the lead singer of the original Platters, I mean this was the guy who was the singer on every one of those 30+ hit records. Unmistakably, he was the REAL Platters.

So here we have it, the original lead singer of the Platters, and a totally bogus group calling themselves the Platters in the same town on the same night. Now I admit it wouldn't be so bad, if at least one member in the New Century Platters was at least maybe a background singer in the original Platters. Not the case here, this bogus group consisted of all young guys and a girl, who would be standing on that stage that night, announcing to the audience, "ladies and gentlemen, here is one of the first hit records we recorded in 1958". Listen, in 1958 the guys were like four years old, while Tony Williams was knocking out hit after hit.

Now here's the kicker of the whole deal. The local newspaper runs a review on both shows. And in the review the reporter makes a statement, "the New Century Platters put on a tremendous show, while another group billing themselves as Tony Williams and the Platters, were a poor excuse for the original Platters". Are you fucking kidding me? You're talking about Tony Williams the original and only lead singer of the Platters. A poor excuse for the original Platters? This reporter should be doing reviews on 4H club meetings, where they were showcasing cows and pigs, instead of reviewing a legendary singer.

It gets better, we finish out the week in Greenville, and head to Fort Walton Beach Florida. We are booked in there for three nights, at a place called the Beachcomber, and right down the street is another club, that is advertising on their marquee, Saturday night the original Coasters.

We were only doing one show a night at the Beachcomber, so that gave me an opportunity to catch the Coasters.

So now you're about to hear how corrupt and how the back room manipulations got over on the public every single time.

We walk into the club, and on the stage is a group calling themselves the Coasters. They are the same fucking group, from Greenville that was calling themselves, the

New Century Platters five days before, only now they're claiming to be the Coasters, and singing all the records that the Coasters had.

It later became known to all that this bogus group, was one of the groups put together by an agent from Virginia called "Philly", strictly to con the public, make money by misleading the club owners and the public, plus riding on the fame of these legendary groups. Sucks, I know, but that is still taking place even today, in venues across America and through out Europe, and they are still getting away with it. Maybe not as much now a days, because of the internet exposing who the real members of the original groups were. But every once in a while, one of these FAKE ass groups will pop up.

One of the biggest back room deals to go sour was this one, that shook the entertainment business to it's core.

The single "Girl You Know It's True" recorded by two guys called "Milli, Vanilli, a German R&B duo from Munich. The group was founded by Frank Farian in 1988 and consisted of Fab Morvan and Rob Pilatus. The group's debut album *Girl You Know It's True* achieved international success and earned them a Grammy Award for Best New Artist on February, 21,1990. Milli Vanilli became one of the most popular pop acts in the late 1980s and early 1990s, with millions of records sold. Their success quickly turned to infamy when Morvan, Pilatus and their agent Sergio Vendero confessed that Morvan and Pilatus did not sing any of the vocals heard on the record. This resulted in the group being stripped of their Grammy Award for Best New Artist.

It was first produced by Jesse Powell and had already been completed before Rob Pilatus and Fab Morvan were recruited. And the producers felt that no efforts should be made to refine Pilatus and Morvan's voices. Farian added his own studio-augmented voice to recordings, using back-up singers to hide the other two members' live voices. In 2011 Morvan claimed that Farian manipulated the two of them by giving them a small advance when he signed them. The pair spent most of it on clothes and hairstyling. Several months later, Farian called them and told them they had to lip sync to some pre-recorded music or, as stated in the contract, repay the advance in full. Once again the public was scammed by another back room deal. Now I want to make it perfectly clear, that I also participated in conning the public one time with some live performance dates. It should be noted that every time I finished a major tour, I was always threatening to quit touring completely. Then after being home for four or five weeks, I got the urge once again to go out on the road and perform. It was actually for three different reasons, one my love of music and two for performing to a live audience, and three for the money. I mean have to be realistic about this folks, the money I was making on the road was incredible to say the least. I used to say at one time, I stay in the greatest hotel suites, eat the best food available, hookup with the best looking women in those towns, and they pay me to do it, not the women of course, but the promoters, and all I have to do was get on the stage and sing.

Well there was one time when I had completed a four month tour, and was sitting on my ass in Fort Lauderdale Florida for five weeks, and I got the bug to get back on the road. One problem though, I had fired the band, so there was no band to go on the road with. All that was left in Florida from that last tour was Blake Marean, one of my roadies, and Jimmy Derease one of the guitar players in the last band. The two of them were actually staying at a local campground in one of my equipment vans. So here's the problem, I need to get back on the road, however, I'm a front man, you know, just a singer, I mean I could play keyboards and guitar if I had to, and Blake didn't play an instrument at all, his job was hauling equipment. And of course with everything I do, it had to be right away, no time to put together a new band, I needed to get my ass back on the road.

So I come up with the brilliant idea, that instead of billing myself as Doc Holiday, we put together a trio and go out to work small clubs in small towns under a band name. But remember there is still a problem because the only two musicians were me and Jimmy. I played keyboard and he played guitar. Now what do we do about a drummer. Okay well here comes the con. First off I name the band High Tech, second I go to a local music store and buy a cheap ass set of drums. My idea was that me and Jimmy would actually play and sing, and what I would do was get Blake to sit behind the drums, but never hit them. I would have a drum machine going out through the system, and have Blake look like he was playing the drums. It even got to the point where I would not let him have drumsticks, he just had brushes in his hand, so in reality although it looked like he was playing, but no one could hear what he was doing.

Sounds insane right? But it worked. We played approximately 14 different clubs in four months, and the public never knew that I was Doc Holiday, and there was an electronic drum machine actually playing the drums. The scam was so good, that in a few clubs, Blake had attracted some fans, and actually got to bed down a groupie in Tallahassee Florida, who thought he was the greatest drummer that she had ever seen. Now remember, he never hit the drums, it was all a total sham. We even gave him the name of Buddy Bitch on the drums.

Well that lasted a few months and I got it out of my system. And when we finally got back to Fort Lauderdale Florida, I put the old band back together, and once again Doc Holiday would ride again.

**HIGH TECH
(DOC HOLIDAY, BLAKE MAREAN,
JIMMY DEREASE)**

Facebook and Other Things That Piss Me Off

The unstoppable man, quite a statement. Well I guess there was a time in my life, in the early beginning of it anyway, that I believe that I was that guy. I truly believe that I could not be stopped from accomplishing anything I set my mind to, and focused on. And in a way I guess I accomplished that. But looking back at it now, that I am in the winter of my life, I'm forced to reflect on the things that I gave up, and the important things in life that I missed. The main thing is, you look back at it all. and try to give it some reason for it all, in other words was it really worth it?

Now back in the day when I first started on this musical journey of mine, the only thing that was on my mind was to make it big, nothing else mattered. And if something got in my way, I would rollover it like a bulldozer, whether it was a business obstacle, a person preventing me from moving forward, or what ever it was, anything, everything and anybody was fair game for destruction if they or it got in the way.

Then after all that shit, you finally make it, you finally become what you been driving for all those years, and your hit with the blunt reality, that it's really not that big of a fucking deal after all. I mean sure fame is cool, the money and the things that money can buy are great, and of course your ego is being fed 24/7.

Yup, all those things are great, but at what cost, that is really the big question. Because in the end when you look back at it, it ain't about how high you got on the ladder of life, I really believe looking back at it today, that it's how much good you did along the way, you know how big a footprint did you leave on the journey, to make it where you needed to be, to feel successful. Because when you reflect back, that's all you're really looking for, is the good thoughts, the happy moments, but instead that whole picture of the past is cluttered with the dark side. Don't get me wrong it wasn't all bad, but if I had to do over again I would do it a lot different.

So I guess this chapter is just gonna be about me ranting and raving about things, that bug me and other bullshit, that goes on in my everyday life these days.

Facebook, now where the fuck did that come from? I never go on Facebook, well actually every once in a while, I will stick my nose into that to take I look. The truth be known, I actually have five different Facebook pages out there, but I have a staff of three girls, that do nothing but maintain those Facebook pages. But as I said, every once in a blue moon, I'll go on Facebook on our sites, and see some of the horse shit that is posted up there by people.

It amazes me, that some people will actually post videos of them singing, and for the most part they are fucking horrible. And then you read the comments underneath the post, and there are people saying like, oh that was beautiful, you have such a great voice, I love that tune. Are you fucking kidding me? That shit was horrible. It's unbelievable, I mean don't people have ears, are they all hard of hearing, or just stupid asses.

Now grant you every once in a while there will actually be a musical video of somebody, that is really good, but the majority of them are hilarious. I called them Facebook idols, and after reading the comments of some of their friends, it is plain to see while they are driven to continue this mental abuse of normal minds out there that love music. I could go on forever with this Facebook crap, but I think I got my point across, and the majority of you out there have to agree with me. Forget about the people that are posting the videos of them dancing and singing, I mean that's strange enough, but the comments below encouraging them, is mind baffling. And a lot of them are actually videotaping themselves with their iPhones or cell phones beating the shit out of a guitar and singing like a wounded pig. I mean some of them are upside down, some of them are sideways, and in a few of them the singer is actually not even in the picture. But in a lot of cases, I guess that is a real blessing.

Another thing that bugs the shit out of me, are people that post videos of them performing in a little small club, or a fucking bowling alley, wherever, and all they are doing is sitting on a stool, beating the hell out of a guitar, and singing some song, I guess that's an original that really nobody wants to fucking hear except the very close family. And then you read the comments below, and you read stuff like," what a great show". Are you fucking kidding me, that's not a show. A show is when you actually see somebody doing something unique, not sitting on a stool, pounding the hell out of a guitar (which by the way most of them can't even play), and once again singing songs that not only does nobody in the audience knows, but to boot, most of the people there, don't want to hear that bullshit to begin with.

Nashville Tennessee, is full of that crap. They call it songwriters nights, and in Nashville, they will actually team up three or four of these characters at one shot, and call it songwriters in the round. So not only are you abused by one idiot sitting on a stool, now you got three or four of them doing it. And you will always get that comment "great show last night". It ain't a fucking show moron. That has always bugged me about Nashville. And to this day you will have hundreds flocking to lower Broadway, to sing all night, for free (that's right most of them don't get paid for that shit, it's those shit hole clubs their way to get free entertainment) with the hopes of being discovered, getting a record contract, and becoming a big star. Well I got news for you, I have yet to see one record executive, or person of power in the music industry, go into one of those dumps on lower Broadway.

And while I'm on the subject of Facebook, here is another thing that bugs the hell out of me. People who post animal abuse pictures, video and news articles. I mean really, what the fuck is the matter with you people.

I have given strict orders to the girls that maintain those Facebook pages for me, to unfriend and block anybody that post that shit to my time line. Stop and think about it, here you have a video of an animal being abused, and some moron is videotaping it. So not only is it sick to do that to a defenseless animal, but you also have an ass hole videoing it, so they can get their 15 minutes of sick fame. And what you do or should I say they do, when they post something like that, is actually get the idiots that 15 minutes of fame.

I know there are some of you out there that say, you are posting it to make us aware. Bullshit, we are already aware that there are some sick mother fuckers out there, and I for one, don't need to be reminded of that by seeing a video of a poor animal being brutalized.

You want to do something good?, you want to make somebody aware?, Post that shit to those damn cops, and do some god damn good with your post, rather than advertising and giving fame to some worthless piece of shit so calledhuman beings.

You're all probably wondering now, what this rant about Facebook, has to do with the music business and my career. Well, when I see some of the shit like I just mentioned, you know the suck ass singers, the pieces of garbage that abused animals, and I see people commenting on those post, adding more fuel to the fire by either agreeing or in some cases, complementing the poster with encouraging, and complementary responses, then that stops me cold in my tracks, and dispels any hope I have for a shred of decency and intelligence left in humanity.

Now don't get me wrong, I am not saying that I am hollier than thou, but I sure as hell will never subject myself to some of the shit I see posted on Facebook.

Moving right along at warp speed, here is another thing that bugs the hell out of me with Facebook, and I'm sure it bugs a lot of you out there, you just don't say anything about it. It's simply, women of all ages posting glamor pictures of themselves on Facebook. I mean really do you really have to do that on Facebook to make yourself feel of value. I mean it's not like you are showing something off that you work your butt off for, you were born with it, you didn't do anything, except be lucky enough to be born with decent looks.

Now I will admit that some of them are actually good-looking, but a lot of them, and excuse me for being blunt, are really middle age road hard and hung out to dry hogs. And there they are doing sexy poses, showing cleavage, of sagging breast I might add, an posing at what they perceived to be some sort of sexy pose. I mean I even saw a few in underwear, you heard me right, panties and bra, with a big ass grin on their face, all for the cause of their vanity.

And that's not the best part. You have to read some of the comments underneath the pictures. You have a bunch of sick degenerate guys that probably couldn't get a date, if their life depended on it and have been jerking off for the past 10 years. And here they are posting in the comments, "your beautiful", "very sexy", and the phrases go on and on. And you look at some of the pictures of these guys complementing these women, and oh my God. You think some of the women were ugly, you gotta check out the guys that are writing the comments. I mean the closest they could come to being attractive to any woman or getting laid, is if they were offering a million dollars to just go and have coffee with them and be seen with them. And then you have the women responding to the comments," oh thank you", "you are so sweet" etc.

    I mean give me a fuckin' break ladies, look at these fucking guys, half of them look like serial killers, and the other half, your left wondering, who was watching the trailer park while they are on the Internet. It cracks me up when I read some of that shit. The truth be known, that is one of the reasons I don't go on Facebook that much. And one of the main reasons, that when I do go on it, I don't stay very long.

Now remember, I did say that some of them were good-looking. But really honey, do you really need to get your 15 minutes of fame, by posting a glamor picture of yourself, on a social media site? If you need attention that bad, then the guys that are posting the comments underneath the pictures, are really not the only sick ones here, are they? I mean let's get real, what do you really get out of posting a glamor picture of yourself on Facebook, to get comments from a bunch of jerk offs, who in reality are probably blowing your picture up, and masturbating to it. Think about it ladies! And who ever the genius was that invented selfies, you should be hung until dead. At lease back in the day they had to stand in front of a mirror and you would see the camera in their hands, AH, but you would also get to see the full body in the picture. Now you only sometimes, see just the face as they are doing a selfie, and you miss the hippo body hidden out of camera range. But even then I bet you would have these jerk off guys commenting, "Oh Beautiful", "I wish I was there with you gorgeous". Oh well, what ever floats your boat kids.

You know, I probably listen to anywhere from 25 to 50 demos a week, sent in by artists that want me and my team to produce them. And yes, I do listen to them all. Well not all the way through on all of them. I do a thing called a needle drop. That's a term that was invented back in the day in the record business, when records were on vinyl, and you would take the turntable needle, and drop it and listen to the first 50 or 60 seconds of the record, or song. So today I still do that, I mean I don't drop a needle on a CD, but I do listen to the beginning part of the song, and into the chorus. If it doesn't grab me right away, I go on to the next one. And out of approximately 200 demos sent in every month, I probably only like two or three artists. The bottom line is, I gotta love the artist, and love the material, and if those two things are not knocking me out of my chair, I wind up passing on the record and artist.

I'm asked time and time again," what are you looking for"? I wish I could answer that question truthfully, but unfortunately I don't have an answer for that. It's really strange, I'm not looking for anything in particular. It's just something that hits me. It's that magic, when the words and the music come together, and the artist becomes a vehicle that delivers the final magic.

Now what bugs the hell out of me, is when you put on a record, and the introduction, you know the instrumental part, is over a minute long. I mean really, you have to wait a minute, to hear the God damn song. An introduction should never be any more than 15 to 20 seconds long. I mean really what are you selling an instrumental part, or are you selling a story, a song, a theme, a thought, and most importantly an artist.

So a word to the wise for all you young untested artist out there. When you're submitting yourself or song to a producer or a record label, get to the meat and potatoes quick, don't bullshit around with your unique guitar playing. We as producers and record labels, don't have that kind of time to kill, listening to hundreds of songs and artist. Give us what you got, and do it quickly. Once you've gotten our attention, then the rest is up to us.

Oh I almost forgot, one important element that comes into play when I'm listening to demos, trying to find what in my opinion is a hit song and a hit artist. Like I said earlier, I get a lot of demos sent to me, and after going through two or 300 of them, I finally hit on one that I think maybe has a shot. When that happens, I usually ask one of my staff to contact the artist and get some more information on them. One of the important things that I ask for is a picture of the artist. Because unfortunately in today's entertainment business the cosmetic looks of the artist plays a big part, if you intend to go to a major label to try to get a recording contract.

As stupid as it sounds, the age of the artist has a lot to do with a major label signing them. Now that doesn't hold true to the complete entertainment industry. Unlike what major-labels think is sell-able, fortunately for us in the music business, the public thinks the opposite. If an artist is good at what they do, age has no bearing on it whatsoever. If you go into a major label, and you're just looking to start a great career, age and looks have very little to do with it. I mean lets face it, Willie Nelson ain't winning no beauty contest.

That being said, to go back to what I was talking about. I would finally hit on an artist that sounded great and had a great song. Now the next thing I asked for is a short bio of the artist, so I can have a little insight of who they are and what they've accomplished so far. I also asked for a picture of the artist, so

I can get some sort of idea of what they look like, and what type of market I could pursue with them.

Now comes the part that completely blows my mind. I'm sold on the song, sold on the artist voice, and sold on the looks. I mean their like 28 to 30 years of age, and the vocal was nice and clear and strong, so in my mind we got a possible project here.

To make a long story short I negotiate an agreement with the artist to produce them, we booked the studio time, and were all set to go. Now mind you up to this point, most of the time I have not spoken to the artist personally.

Well the day of the session, the artist shows up, and that's when I discovered that the picture that they sent in was taken 30 years ago, and the demo was recorded 30 years ago. Now remember I told you that age does not scare me when it comes to an artist. However at this point we were totally misled. So now I'm faced with the dilemma of how do we make this act and this song into something commercially competitive. That's when the producer comes really into play. It's my job to take whatever I got and mold it into something that radio will embrace and the fans will be able to connect with.

If I am ever to be remembered as a producer, I hope it's for that part of my career. I was able to successfully mold what ever I had into a commercially competitive product. And sure enough all of them did not become superstars, but all of them were elevated to a higher level in the industry, then they were before I produced them.

I have said this 1 million times during my career," you could have the sweetest apples in the world, but if they are buying peaches, your screwed". As a producer, it was and is my job to know what they are buying at that particular point in time.

Doc with Doug, Terri and Bobby Bradley at QUAD Studios Nashville, TN

Doc in deep thought listening to a playback on what he just created

Friends, Players and Internet Idols

Throughout my career I came in contact with many many people, some became friends, and some became enemies. And in the beginning of my career, the circle or entourage that surrounded me, was extremely large, but as I grew older I decreased that circle into a very small diameter of what it once was.

For some very strange reason I always attracted lawyers, doctors, and professional people, who actually had nothing to do with the music industry, but for some reason were all connected in one way or another to music, not the industry, but to the art of music. Meaning in one way shape or form they were all big fans of music in general.

Now that's not to say that people connected with the music industry were not a part of that circle, because they, also were in there.

So in this chapter, I am going to get into some of those relationships, and basically what I got out of the friendship, and also what they got out of it. Because really folks any relationship that takes place on any level, one person is always using the other person involved in a relationship for one thing or another.

I want to start off with a guy I met, who was, and still, is an extremely high powered attorney, not in the music industry, but a personal injury attorney. This guy was not only brilliant at what he did, he was also a law professor at a high rated ivy league university. But again I have to say this guy was high powered. You may remember the BP oil spill off the coast of Louisiana, that was settled in the billions of dollars. One of the biggest settlements ever recorded in the history of our judicial system. This man was one of the lead attorneys in that lawsuit that came out a winner. So when I say he was high-powered, that is far from an exaggeration, but he also had an extreme passion for music, and I think in some strange way we became friends. I think in a strange way, I was in awe of his talent as an attorney, and he was also in awe of my talent and position in the music industry, so there was a mutual respect for the both of us.

I will refer to him as Jeffrey, because being an attorney, he will probably sue me for what I have to say. Jeffrey was a very short man in stature, which gave him what I considered a Napoleonic complex, meaning a little guy that wanted to be a big guy as far as physical aspects were concerned. It even went as far as me giving him the nickname of Smurf, which in his circle was unheard of because of the respect he demanded, and got because of his accomplishments in the field of law. His passion for music and the joy he received by being around people connected with music, became almost his drug of choice and I guess I was a connection to that music scene in some small way that he embraced somewhat.

We both had a habit of badgering and teasing each other, which amazed everybody connected with Jeffrey, that I could get away with, and probably left a lot of them in shock, that I could get away with it. But on the other hand he would rib me constantly, and that would shock my circle of friends, that he could get away with it.

Being as successful as he was, he lived in a very big house in Virginia Beach, and was married to a sweetheart named Susie. She was totally the opposite from the both of us personality wise, and I guess in sort of a strange way tolerated mine and his friendship and of course our actions towards each other. So I will close this segment by simply saying, Jeffrey has done a lot for me over the years, much more than I ever did for him. But in a weird way, I think I became entertainment for him and also he became entertainment for me. But to this day I have to admit, I have, and always will have, the ultimate respect for his talent and ability to be able to handle any situation that arose, and without a doubt in my opinion he is an Einstein of an attorney. BUT HE'S STILL A GOD DAMN SMURF TO ME!!!

Jeffrey Before Doc Holiday

Jeffrey After Doc Holiday

Enter, Bill Reid!, Bill has probably been a friend of mine for at least, I would say 25 years. Just a little background on Bill, he is a very high profile concert promoter, physically he is a sharp looking man, a brilliant businessman, and mentally, he is constantly at the top of his game.

Bill was actually the guy that introduced me to Jeffrey, and Jeffrey always said that Bill had a scattered focus, because Bill had 1000 things going on in his mind and life at the same time.

Bill in my opinion, was an idea guy, meaning he was constantly coming up with different angles to do different things. It was sort of like if you could imagine, Bill walking into a room and saying to me, "I got an idea Doc, we raise tuna fish, and feed them nothing but celery, onions and mayonnaise, this way you have instant tuna salad". In reality he never actually said that to me, but I would not be shocked if one day he came in and laid that on me.

I have to mention this one incident, and he may get mad at me about telling this, but this little incident with me and Bill happened, concerning the Grammy awards one year.

You see Bill, had a lot of involvement

with the band the Wailers. He had managed them for a while, put concerts on with them, set up tours for them, you name it, Bill did it with the Wailers. Those of you who do not know who the Wailers are, they were Bob Marley's backup band.

So anyway getting to the story of the Grammy awards. One year the band the Wailers were nominated for a Grammy award, and Bill at the time was managing them. Now a Grammy award is a big deal in the entertainment industry, so this was a huge lick for Bill. But you also have to keep in mind that managing the Wailers was insane to say the least. I mean these guys had more drama and problems than anyone could ever possibly imagine. To put it in my own opinion, that whole Wailers scene was fucked up, once again in my opinion, you have to constantly wonder if it was even worth it getting involved in any way shape or form, but Bill was there, through thick and thin, so I guess to him it was important.

Okay now back to the Grammy award thing, it seemed that everybody in the Wailers got free tickets to the Grammy awards that year, and each one was allowed to bring a guest, because like I said the band was nominated for a Grammy.

Okay, here comes the drama and bullshit, that was always tied up with the Wailers, that I told you about. It seems that one of the members of the band, was in prison doing time for a serious crime, when the Grammy awards were held. Now comes Bill with one of his a great ideas, he's going to take the two tickets allotted to the member of the band that was in prison, and attend the Grammy awards as that member, and to top it all off, bring his 17-year-old daughter so she can enjoy the experience of Grammy awards. Now remember Bill is supposed to be this guy in the band, who happens to be in prison. Confused yet, wait it gets better. The band the Wailers for those of you who do not know, are all black from Jamaica, and Bill is white, and his daughter has blonde hair and blue eyes. So number one how could he possibly pull this shit off.

Bill called me up one night while I am at my recording studio, and informs me that he has a plan to pull this insane idea of his off. I said "Bill are you fucking nuts?, You have to show an ID to get the tickets, plus the fact, somebody in the Grammy organization, sooner or later is going to realize that you're not black, your a white guy from Virginia, and as far from a reggae keyboard player in the Wailers as you can get".

Right now it really starts to get crazy with this idea that Bill had. So he called me up one night while I'm at the studio, and it's like 12 midnight. The only problem with Bill's complete scheme of entering the Grammys as one of the members of the Wailers, is that you will need identification in order to get the tickets for the awards, and to attend all parties associated with the Grammy s.

Now Bill knows that I fooled around a lot with a computer program called Photo-shop. And anyone that knows that program, knows you could practically do anything with it, or alter anything.

So here we go, 12 midnight, in the recording studio, and me and Bill sitting in front of a Macintosh computer, while I create two fake IDs, one for Bill, and one for his daughter, who like I said was only 17 years old at the time, and had to be 21 to attend all the Grammy dinners and parties.

So after five hours of work that night, it is now a little after 5 AM, and we had the two IDs. We actually had a machine at the studio that would seal them in plastic, so it looked like a real ID.

Now comes the real test. Bill heads out to Los Angeles, to the Grammy awards, presented his fake ID, and lo and behold they give him the tickets to the Grammy awards. Now it gets really insane, Bill and his daughter walked the red carpet into the Grammy awards, as Bill portraying the member of the Wailers, and no one, I mean no one, questioned it. I mean let's face it guys, here's a white guy Bill Reid, saying he is nominated for Grammy and claiming to be the black reggae keyboard player of the Wailers, and not one single person from the Grammy awards takes up on the switch.

On the red carpet, one very famous record label head, walked up to Bill and said, "so you're in the Wailers" and of course Bill answered, "yea I'm the keyboard player", and the record label head just looked at him and said, "RIGHT!", With a big smile on his face.

Okay here's the kicker, they are doing a tribute to Bob Marley that night, and someone from the Grammy awards comes up to Bill and says, "hey, you know were doing a big tribute to Bob Marley tonight, and Bob's son Ziggy is performing doing the televised portion of the Grammy awards"," so I guess you will be up there performing with them". Bill doesn't lose of beat, and looks at the girl and says "I guess so". Well right now I'm back in Virginia, and Bill called me and told me what happened concerning performing at the Grammy's. I said Bill "are you fucking crazy, you're gonna blow your whole cover man".

So Bill and his daughter go to the Grammy party before the awards. Bill walks in and a lady from the Grammy Association, walks up to Bill and says, "oh your with the Wailers, did you get your Grammy medallion yet?, And Bill says, no, so they take him in one of the side rooms, and actually give him a Grammy Award medallion for being nominated, and then they asked if they could take a picture of him and his girlfriend! Okay remember, Bill is with his 17-year-old daughter, and the nit wits at the Grammy awards, not only don't figure out that Bill is in no way is a part of the Wailers, but now they think as his 17-year-old daughter is his girlfriend. So today, if you walk into Bill's office there it is, hanging on the wall, the Grammy award medallion. And once again another memory of insanity with myself and Bill Reid. OH yea, through all of this shit, It should be noted that I was on the board of governors for the Grammy awards. How's that for dedication and respect for my position on the Grammy board! I could go on and on about some of the escapades, of myself and Bill, but unfortunately there are many other maniacs that surrounded me, (the number one maniac), that I have to get to in this book.

Bill Reid Before Doc Holiday

Bill Reid After Doc Holiday

Now it's time to introduce to you, a guy name Hot Dog Tony from Norfolk Virginia.

He had a little hot dog stand, that he claimed to be legendary in Virginia, and sold hot dogs on a lot that was actually in the ghetto part of Norfolk. He was introduced to me by a guy that I was doing a television show with, who was called Henry the Bull, who was a local radio disc jockey celebrity.

I immediately gave him the nickname hot

dog Tony, and one day Henry The Bull bought him over to my recording studio. It didn't take me long to figure out that hot dog Tony was full of shit. First off he claim to be a jazz drummer, and said he had his own recording studio. So the night that Henry brought him over to the studio, he brought some CD's with him that he recorded.

I remember putting one of the CD's on in the studio, and it was unbelievable. It sounded like a cat walking on the keyboard of the piano, and the drums were the worst I had ever heard in my 50+ years in the recording industry. I said to him, "what the fuck is this shit"?, And he said to me "it's avaunt-grade jazz, you have to wait for the moment". Are you fucking kidding me, this was the worst shit I ever heard in my life. And without a doubt, he was the worst drummer that I ever heard in my career. But deep down he was a good soul, he just bull shitted about everything, you couldn't believe a word he said, more or less he was a perpetual liar. But a harmless liar. He didn't really try to hurt anybody, he lied to make himself look bigger than he actually was, and more talented then he was, and of course more successful than he actually was.

So one day I surprised him and showed up at his hot dog stand, that was a trip in itself. Here was this old beat up trailer that was probably 5' x 6' in size, dirty as hell, and once again in the heart of a ghetto district, and he was selling hot dogs out of it.

So anyway we were talking outside, he had like a little picnic table out there, and I said, so where is this recording studio. He said right there, and I looked over and it was a run down garage. I said so let me see it. Now Henry had already warned me ahead of time, he said "wait to you see the studio, it's like the dwelling of a serial killer". I walk into this garage with hot dog Tony, and I was in total awe. Here was a two-car garage, that was run down to hell on the outside, and surrounding the garage was a bunch of rusty old beat up worthless cars.

He opened the door and I walked into the studio, or what he claim to be a studio, and I'm telling you right now, there wasn't enough room to walk once you got inside. There was all kinds of junk piled up to the ceiling. There was a life-size Michael Jackson cut out standing up, that he had dressed up with a hat and a tie, shit all over the floor, all kinds of wires hanging from the ceiling, a bunch of religious paintings hanging on the wall, huge stuffed animals all over the place, I mean it was a fucking mess, in between all the junk, was a baby grand piano, a set of drums, and hundreds of broken down instruments, tables, chairs and couches.

It was so obvious to see that this guy was a hoarder. Now comes the shock of the whole deal, I can not walk into this room because all of the junk stuff that was cluttering the whole place. So I got in a few feet and I was stop by walls of garbage, and I said, "where do you sit down"?, And he said there's a couch right over there under all that stuff. So we moved a bunch of crap off, and sure enough there was a couch there. Oh I forgot to tell you he had strings and strings of Christmas lights hanging up all over this place. When I finally made it to the couch I realized, that this guy was living in this garage, there was pillows and blankets on the couch. And I said in amazement at that point, "do you live here", and he responded, "yea, I want to be close to my music". I said, are you fucking kidding me?. I said where's your bathroom, where's your shower?. And he walks me out around the back of the garage on the outside, and he's got a garden hose hanging on a rod, and that was a shower, and remember it was outside, That means he would take a shower in a snow storm, It was just a garden hose, and for a bathroom, he had an old beat up port a John that smelled like shit to the high heavens. This was all surreal, it was like a trip to the twilight zone, and what made it worse, he claimed he was wealthy. He actually used to say to everybody "I have more money than God, "now you're getting the picture that everything that came out of this guy's mouth was bullshit.

Now comes the icing on the cake. You remember I told you that he had his property right in the heart of a ghetto, and he lived in a run down garage, surrounded by junk cars and trash, and his hot dog stand was a homemade beat up trailer, that looked like a food poisoning Castle. But hot dog Tony claimed it to be legendary.

Well one day the city of Norfolk hit him with a court order, demanding him to get rid of the trash and the junk cars, and a huge rotten 30 foot wooden boat that was setting on the property. Plus the health department had hit him with a ton of health violations in the hot dog trailer, and through it all hot dog Tony disputed every criticism that the city issued him. I mean, he actually went to court and fought to keep that junk on his property calling it all treasures. Guess what sport fans, he lost big time. They gave him 30 days to clean it up, or he would be fine $1000 a day.

It got so bad, that the city said the property was an eyesore. Now can you imagine that, an eyesore in the middle of a ghetto, how bad is that.

Well to make a long story short, in order to get him out of there, the city of Norfolk, took his property away from him under the eminent domain law, and tore everything down, and just left a vacant lot, with green grass growing.

Of course hot dog Tony, told everyone that the city had bought his property from him to build a fire station, which was a lie, as everything was that came out of his mouth.

Hot dog Tony had probably paid over the past 15 years of having that property close to $400,000 in payments. The city of Norfolk gave him $160,000.00 when they took the property away from him.

Well now hot dog Tony is without a place to live, so what does he do, he moves in with his mother, that's right you heard me, the guy that is bullshitting to everyone, that he has more money than God, at age 60 plus, moves in to Mama's house. But the question remains why did he do that? He had $160,000 that the city gave him, so he finally had the money he was claiming to everyone that he had all along, and according to all the stories that he told me about his mother, this woman was a real whack job, a snake in the grass when it came to how she treated him.

One story he told me about her, knocked me out. You see back in the day during the draft, all guys 18 years old were forced to go into the military, by being what they called drafted. Now hot dog Tony did not want to be drafted so instead, he was going to join the Air Force, which everybody knew was never in harm's way. I mean that's why they called it the chair force. You're really didn't do anything and you never really carried a gun or got involved in firefights.

So hot dog Tony had two choices, run to Canada, like many guys did during those times, to avoid being drafted in the Army or the Marines, where he could get his ass killed, or joined the Air Force.

Now here's the kicker of the whole deal. The loving mother received a letter from the government, stating that Tony could not be drafted. So in reality he never had to join the military, they couldn't draft him. However that dear sweet mother hid the letter from Tony, and never told him about it, so hot dog Tony joined the military, never knowing that he was deferred from the draft. He found it out 25 years later, when he found the letter that was written to him, that his mother never gave him or told him about. How's that for motherly love.

Now the hook of the whole story is, remember hot dog Tony was thrown out of his property, and being the hoarder that he was, he had no place to put all his junk. And there was no way he was going to throw any of it away, and believe me there was tons of junk and garbage that no one could possibly imagine existed.

Now Mama owned a little house in Virginia Beach, and Tony moves in there claiming he was there to take care of Mama, when the reality of everything was, he was looking for a place to put all his junk and all the junk cars, and in the back of his mind he thought Mama, owned the house free and clear, and sooner or later she was going to kick the bucket, and leave him the house. (She was eating Oxycontin pills, that she claimed was for pain like M&Ms) little did Tony know at the time, she was a bigger bullshit artist then he was. She was in debt up to her ass, and had the house mortgage to the hills.

I can remember hot dog Tony called me one time is said, Mama, signed a will that hot dog Tony had downloaded from the Internet, and left him the house. I said, idiot, she don't own the God damn house moron, why don't you let her leave you the statue of liberty and the Brooklyn bridge while you're at it.

The bottom line was, taking into consideration all of hot dog Tony's faults, he basically was a good soul deep down inside, and he had a tremendous passion for music. I mean music of all kinds. Even though he couldn't play a lick (I mean it was basically pretty terrible), he still loved all kinds of music and he was extremely passionate about it, and I think that's one of the main reasons that I stuck in there with him.

Sure, he was the ultimate loser, but in reality that was basically all his own fault. You see he never finished anything. He would start out with such great energy on any project, and then quit right before it was finished, and rely on bullshit to make it seem like the project was completed.

I think hot dog was the only guy in history, that claimed bankruptcy, and the bankruptcy court did not want to confiscate one thing of all that junk he had collected, that he swore was treasure. But through it all, for some strange reason, I felt compelled to include him on many many, musical events that I participated in. And I guess in some way those times when I included him, allowed him to live the dream that he could never achieve on his own, of being a musician. So during that part of the whole relationship between me and hot dog Tony, I guess in a strange way it was worthwhile for me to include him in as many major events that I could.

Because once again, he basically was a great guy, but the stories that he told me, about how he was raised and treated by his father and mother, which in all likelihood was the reason he turned out to be the way he was. Like I said, good guy, meant well, just had a serious problem in living in the reality.

I could go on and on about hot dog Tony, I mean there was enough there to have another book, the size of war and peace, and never even scratched the surface of some of the turmoil that this man created through his actions. So I will close with this, hot dog Tony, in a strange but real way, you were a friend, and may you rest in peace my friend.

Well now we come to a thing I like to call, Internet idols. People who post videos of themselves singing with a karaoke machine or even them playing a very poor guitar and singing original songs that they wrote, that really nobody wants to hear to begin with, and then you get the comments underneath all their friends saying, what a beautiful voice, or wow you really are good, when in reality they suck! I mean some of them are the worst fuckin' thing I have ever heard in my life, but on any given day you can go to Facebook, and get brutalized by some of the shit so called singers that's on there.

Oh, and then you also have the mothers of these little kids pushing them to be singers, when in reality nine out of 10 of them are terrible. But if you watch real closely, you will hear the mothers say that the kids are really into what they're doing, but the mothers are living their dream through their kid. Really, just let the kid be a kid, instead of dressing them up in country garb, giving them stupid ass names, like little Miss country, or country sweetheart, and the list goes on and on. Bottom line is they can't sing.

But if you ask the mother, she says, my child wants to do this, sure because your Dragging them all around all the place, making them think that they're going to be big country music stars, when once again in reality all you're doing, is robbing them from their childhood, so the parents can feed their own egos at the child's expense. Really when you think of it, this is really so sad. Little girls and little boys instead of playing with their friends and doing normal kids stuff, are being dragged all over the place to sing and then, a video of them is posted to face book, so the parents can read the comments of all their friends saying oh how great their child is. Come on you must have ears people, nine out of 10 of these kids can't sing a note, and in no way will ever pursue a career as a country music singer,. And if they did they would fall flat on their ass.

You know you talk about mothers that dragged her kids to the little beauty pageants, this is just about the same. It ain't about the kids, it never was, it is about the loser mothers that have to revert to this kind of bullshit, just so they can justify their existence, and in some way, make up for themselves being total losers in life.

Now don't get me wrong, I'm not saying that everything or every artists on the Internet sucks. Every once in a while you come across one that has real talent. Now I will admit that I rarely go on Facebook, but when I do, the majority of what I see and hear is brutalizing to my eyes and ears. But like I said every once in a while you come across that diamond in the rough.

Case in point, is what we found on Facebook, and they turned out to be fabulous talents. They were both singer songwriters and both were different in every way, yet they were both country.

One was named Bob Randall. He is an older guy and had been in music for probably 40+ years. But misdirected in everything he tried to do as far as recording was concerned. So now we reach today's market which is totally different, than when it was when he broke into the business. Back in his day, it was real country music, something they call traditional country now, and fortunately for him the industry had changed, to a thing they call country pop or country rock. However that being said, there is still a huge audience out there that is still wanting traditional country. Now that leaves the door wide open for a guy like Bob Randall. And if one thing is certain in the music industry is not how you sound, but are you different, and Bob Randall 40 years ago was not different, but in today's marketplace he's totally different.

So we recorded him using his original material which was reflective of country music 40 years ago, and we use modern recording techniques, to make him sound commercially competitive in today's marketplace.

We labeled him Bob the real deal Randall, and sure enough he takes off like wildfire. People are loving him around the world. He wins two Global music awards and makes it to the voting ballot of the Grammy awards, but he has that look, that worn-out country look, and his songs are about real life, stuff you can relate to. Because after all folks, real country music is three chords and the truth. It's that simple, and that's what Bob Randall is all about. No pretty boy face, doesn't look like a model, but he delivered what a huge part of the country music audience around the world, was still clamoring for all along.

Bob is definitely on his way, and what better way for him to finally do his career, the only way he ever really knew how to do it. Real country music, Bob the real deal Randall. Let's hope it's not to late for Mr. Randall to leave his foot print in country music.

Bob "The Real Deal" Randall

Well one day my staff is surfing the Internet looking for artists for an upcoming session. I myself, rarely go on the Internet, because like I said, most of the artists I see on there are brutal to say the least.

Lynda, my office manager comes across a guy that she thinks is somebody I would like to hear. So I told her okay send me some information on him. She responded, the only problem is, he's from New South Wales Australia. Well not only is it expensive to record with me, but to fly from Australia to Nashville, I mean really, that's a lot of damn money. But I said okay send me the stuff and let me listen to him.

So she sends me a link to his post, and I immediately listen to what he had up there. In short, the guy was awesome, he was both a brilliant songwriter, as well as being a killer singer. His name was and still is, Steve Condon, and if you can imagine, he was a cross between Roy Orbison as a singer, and Jimmy Webb as a songwriter. I mean to tell you this guy was not a three chord genius, some of the chord changes he had in his songs, were totally brilliant, and his melody lines flowed like no tomorrow. Now remember I told you he was from Australia, so we have to figure out how we can cut one song on this guy, to test it on radio, and not break his bank doing it.

So I came up with a plan, to cut the basic

rhythm tracks at Sony with my "A" team, and then send the sound files over to Australia, and have him sing the song in another studio over there called Impromptu Music, and then send all the files back to me in Nashville, were I would reassemble it all and do all the overdubs including the background singers.

Well here we go, we send the sound files over to Australia, and I instruct the studio over there how I want his vocal done, no re verb, no echo, no EQ, I want it done totally raw. To make a long story short, they did a hell of a job over in Australia, and when we got the sound files back, they were perfect in every sense of the word.

The name of the song was "There is still lots of country in the boy", and to say it was a radio smash would be an understatement. The song stayed on the charts for over three months, with six weeks of that in the top five. So we definitely had a hot property with Steve. The next thing you know, he flew to Nashville and recorded in EP of six songs, wound up winning two Global music awards, and made it to the voting ballots of the Grammy awards. Which just goes to show you, ya never really know when you're going to find that diamond in the rough.

STEVE CONDON

You know when you're on the road on tour, you meet a lot of people, some are memorable, and some are not. Case in point, you know for the life of me I don't know why I keep saying Case In Point, because I don't have a fuckin' clue what it means, but it sounds good. So anyway, case in point, we are on tour playing at Caesars Palace in Las Vegas, and one night while I was walking to the dressing room, sometimes people recognize you from being on the stage. And as you're walking to the stage to get ready to perform, people would come up to you and introduce themselves, and most of the time you just robotically say, hello or how you doing.

Well one night at Caesars Palace I was headed towards the dressing room walking through the casino, and I guess maybe 15 or 20 people stop me and introduced themselves, and I once again robotically acknowledged it without paying any mind to it whatsoever.

Fast-forward four weeks after that date. We are booked in a place called the Alabama Show Palace in Montgomery Alabama, and the tour buses rolled up to the motel where we were staying, and we all checked into our rooms. Well, I was not in my room more than 30 minutes when the phone rings and it's the front desk, and the girl says, Sheriff Lenny is here to see you. So right away in my brain, I'm saying to myself, what the fuck happen now, did one of the guys get busted, they found dope on the bus, I'm in kind of a panic mode. So I said to the girl at the front desk I'll send my road manager Blake down, and she comes back and says no he has to see you. Now I'm really shiting in my pants, I'm thinking we really fucked up someplace. So I head downstairs to find out what the problem was, and sure enough here is this Sheriff in full uniform standing there. I walk up to him a little nervous, I have to admit, and before I get to him he sticks his hand out and says, Doc, how are you doing.

Well it turns out that there really wasn't any problem at all, it seemed that this guy had met me three weeks ago, at Caesars Palace and introduced himself to me while I was walking through the casino. So in short to him it was a memorable meeting, but to me, it was just another handshake on the way to the stage to do my job. And actually that was really commonplace. You know you got so much on your mind when you're getting ready to go on stage that you are oblivious to everything else around you, and in a strange way you just kind of go through the motions.

However that is not always the case, there are many many times that some of those chance meetings became very memorable to me.

I remember 55 years ago from the time

I'm writing this book, I was in a little small bar in Manhattan New York, and I ran into a guy who was a drummer from the United Kingdom. We both really were kinda just starting out then, we had a few drinks and talked about music and what we intended to do with our careers. He had told me he had just gotten into a band, and they were getting ready to come over to the United States. He never mentioned the bands name. I guess we talked for a couple of hours and we said goodbye, and that was probably the whole deal, nothing really exciting just a chance meeting with another musician in New York.

But for some strange reason I remember that night, although I have to admit it wasn't very hard to remember it, because that guy was Ringo Starr from the band the Beatles. So one year after that meeting that band changed the world.

I never saw him or spoke to him again, then one night in 2017, 55 years later, I get an email from a manager named Wayne, and he said that Ringo Starr was coming into town, to do a concert with his Ringo Starr All-Star band, and if I was interested, Ringo would like to have me meet him backstage and say hello.

Well naturally without giving it a second thought, I was on my way down there, and all the way down I couldn't believe that he remembered that meeting 55 years ago. At the time, now, my health was getting really bad, and I had lost the ability to walk any great distance, so when I did go out, I had a caretaker that traveled with me, and I might add, I road in a little electric scooter, but there was no way I was not going to make this meeting with Ringo.

I arrived at the concert hall and was met by his manager Wayne, and he led us backstage. Now remember it's been 55 years since I have seen this guy. And Ringo comes out of the dressing room, and sticks his hand out and says, Doc!

Two minutes into the conversation, and it was like a rewind to 55 years ago. The conversation was great to say the least. We talked about that night, and how memorable it was to the both of us, with neither of us knowing that it was memorable. It was a great meeting, and it was good to see him again, and although there were people taking pictures all around us, me and him were lost in our conversation the way we were so long ago. And as we said our goodbyes, Ringo walked away and turned to me and said "I'll see you again in 55 years My friend". I think we both knew that meeting would never happen.

Doc Holiday and Ringo Starr

Doc and Ringo remembering the past

Before I end this chapter, I have to mention the latest thing, Internet radio. As of the time of writing this book, there are probably 5000 Internet radio stations or shows. I mean if you have a laptop computer that has a microphone, that's all you need to get on one of these sites, and have your own radio show, broadcast worldwide.

Now in my opinion, I venture to say, that 98% of these so-called radio shows are fucking bullshit. I mean really folks, just think about it, who the fuck in this day in age, with television and DVDs, plus a family, sits the fuck at home in front of a computer, with fucked up little speakers, and listen to a God damn radio program.

I'll tell you who, a handful of so-called recording artist, that label themselves "indie artist", and I might add cannot get their music played on terrestrial radio stations. So in short, what these artists do is contact the Internet radio station through the computer and send them an MP3 of their music, and asked them to play their fucked up music, that no one else in the world will play in a legitimate market. So what you have is a handful of people, and I mean a handful, and what ever so-called recording artists that have convinced the station owner to play their shit music. Now I don't know about you, but that sounds like something I would love to do at night after busting my ass working all day. **NOT!!!!!!**

Now remember I said 98% of the station suck, and are total bullshit. However that being said, there are a few that I have run into personally, that are actually run like a professional radio station.

One is called Country Sound Machine broadcasting out of North Carolina, and the main disc jockey is a guy called Tom Barstow. Now this guy has his shit together. He plays all the hits, the major artists as you would expect, and every once in a while, he will throw in a new up and coming artist. I mean to tell you this guy is a professional in every sense of the word, the show is polished and his delivery is second to none.

There is also a girl named Debbi Scott, and she broadcasters her show from the state of Florida, in the United States, along with her husband Jon. They called their show, The Debbi Scott Radio Network, and what makes them unique, is of course they play the hits by major artists, but they also play some of the obscure songs recorded by major artists that don't normally get radio airplay. In the entertainment business they are called album cuts. Now the both of them Debbi and Jon, are as professional as it gets, and I might add as honest as it gets. However, every once in a while they will fall prey, to some so-called "indie" artists, and play that shit that no legitimate radio station in the world would play, but Debbi will try and catch it quick and deleted it from the play lists, and try not to offend the artists doing it, when in reality the only reason the artist is listening to their show, is because Debbi is gracious enough to play that crap to begin with.

Well, enough about Internet radio, oh yea, I forgot to tell you, the artist don't make shit being played on those 5,000 plus internet stations. Oh sure they say they pay streaming royalties, which in layman's terms, means if you're play 10,000 times you'll make two dollars. And the beat goes on.

No Big Deal, Just Stories

You know there was a bunch of stuff that happen in my lifetime, some were important, some were not. A lot of people drifted in and drifted out, some were important, some were not. But all of them and everything that happened, were all memorable in one way or another, and those events and people are all worth remembering, because that is what made me what I am today. The accumulation of everything that went on in my lifetime, would play a major part in the development of myself as a human being. Yes, I grant you some of it was bad influences, but even those influences, mixed with the good ones created Doc Holiday. So what you're going to read in this chapter, is really just a lot of random stories of a few of the things that happened in my lifetime.

I can remember back when I was living on the island, Caribou in Canada, like I had told you in an earlier chapter, I was starting to get itchy feet to get back into the music business, but once again living on an island, it didn't give me much opportunity to meet new artists.

So one day I had this problem with the basement in the house, there was water seeping in, not a lot of water but it was kind of damp down there. So I called a local handyman to come over and take a look at it, and see what he could do about the problem. His name was Wayne Douglas, and he was from the mainland in Nova Scotia, Canada. Well he came over and took a look, and suggested I put a sub pump down there, just in case the water did start to pour in, that pump would take it out and nothing would be damaged.

The floor in the basement was solid concrete, so he said he had to make a small pit in order to put the pump in, and the pit had to be lower than the rest of the floor, so the water would drain into it. Well he gave me a price on doing it, and I hired him to do the job.

He showed up the next day with a partner of his, named Tim. What I have to tell you right now that both these guys were short, you know that they were small, and they were going to tear up this concrete floor that was probably 24 inches thick. So after a lot of noise and a lot of hammering, I went downstairs to take a look at how they were progressing, and sure enough they were getting it done.

While I was down there, Wayne had noticed that there was a bunch of studio recording equipment I had stacked up in the corner of the basement. It was basically equipment that I wasn't using, but wanted to keep. It was then that he informed me, that he was a singer-songwriter, and it was his dream to actually record one of his songs. I remember telling him, well let me hear what you got, and maybe I can help you. Well it didn't take him long, he went out to his van, and came back with a guitar.

So here we are sitting in my basement, with a concrete floor all torn up, and this guy Wayne singing some of his original songs. To be honest with you, this damn guy was pretty good. I mean he was kind of folk orientated, and all of his songs, were about where he lived, and the people that live there and events that happen there, and that made them pretty unique.

So over the next five or six weeks, I got a chance to listen to all of Wayne's songs, and got to know him pretty good in the process. There was even one night when I traveled to see him perform. He was doing a little single act at a small neighborhood bar in a place called, Pugwash, Nova Scotia. A different experience for this city boy for sure, but I must say it was kind of refreshing, to witness that down-home atmosphere.

Well anyway, like I said, I got to know Wayne pretty good, and discovered that his lifelong dream was to go to the United States, and cut a record of one of his original songs. But what stopped him all these years, was knowing, number one where to go, and number two securing the funds to record in the states.

It just so happened that at the time, Wayne was living with a girl, or I should say a woman, that he was also dating, who offered to put up the money for Wayne to come to the United States and record. Naturally he took her up on the offer, and before you know it, myself, Wayne and Tim were on our way to Virginia, for him to cut his first record on one of his original songs. The record came out pretty good, and we all return back to Canada, with Wayne and his recording in hand.

During that trip I got to know Wayne and Tim even more, and it seemed that this broad that he was living with was very controlling, but then again as our friendship went on, I realized that Wayne was not only controlled by her, but by every other woman he had ever had a relationship with. I mean he was that kind of a guy. I also found out then that Tim, had absolutely no training whatsoever on how to deal with adulthood. Don't get me wrong now, the two guys were great guys, but they had their faults as we all do.

When you first looked at Tim, it looked like he was raised by wolves. I mean really, his hair was wild and look like it had never been washed or cut, and combed. And I won't even go into his table manners, because they were nonexistent, but that all put aside, he was really a great kid, and he helped Wayne out a lot. You know, carrying his equipment in helping him get set up. I think Tim, just wanted to be included in something, because with further investigation, it became clear that he had no family life whatsoever.

So anyway like I said we returned to Canada, and Wayne and Tim both were on cloud nine. I mean they had gotten there first taste of what it was like in the states, and their first real involvement in the music business.

And like I said earlier, this broad that Wayne was living with, immediately attempted to take control and bring him down off of the high he was on. Her favorite saying to him was, "you got your dream", and that was her way of saying, now forget about everything else and get back to what you were doing, and the way you were. But I'll tell you right now, that was not going to happen. Long story short, Wayne left her, moved to Virginia, and brought Tim with him.

The first thing I did with Tim, was get his haircut, and get him to wash, oh right, there was another thing, Timmy had never brushed his teeth, and I remember the first time he did it, Jesus Christ, it was a bloodbath. But slowly we were transforming him from Wolf boy to a human being. My next thing with Tim would be to teach him how to drive a car, and believe it or not after about two weeks , he became a pretty good driver. So it was off to get him is driver's license, it was then that I found out he didn't know how to read. So after we finish working on that part of him, and we worked for about three months teaching him basic reading skills, you know just enough so he could navigate around the world and at least read the traffic signs. Well after that, we took him back to get a drivers license, only this time we made sure they gave him the test orally, and he passed it.

So now Wayne and Tim are doing pretty good. Wayne was working on his music, and Tim now look like a normal human being. Wayne made a couple of trips to Nashville, and he was actually performing in the Virginia area. But along came another relationship with a controlling broad, only this time he took it one step beyond normal. He married the broad.

I could go on forever with this saga of Wayne and Tim, but after a while they both went back to Canada, Wayne just packed his stuff up one day, never told his new wife anything, and just left.

Today, as of the writing of this book, Tim is now working being a traffic guard on the roads in Canada, and Wayne is a painter in

Alberta Canada, and I'm sure he looks in the mirror every day and wonders what it would have been, if he continued with his music. To this day I still remain friends with both Wayne and Tim and speak to them often on the phone. Wayne is still pursuing his music as best he can, but guess what, now he met a woman from the Philippines on an online dating site, yup you guessed it, he went over there and married her. I will say he does seem happy, and I of course I am happy for him, but you never can tell, one of these days you may hear a guy on the radio named Wayne Douglas.

WAYNE DOUGLAS AND TIM (The Hawk)

Now picture this, I have a great recording studio in Virginia called the Power Plant, and it is part of my organization called the Holiday Music Group, which encompasses not only recording, but concert promotion, booking, management, publishing, you name it we did it.'

And everything is doing great, I had a great staff of seven people, and we were making a ton of money, the only problem was I got bored. So I came up with an idea to have a weekly half-hour late-night television show, you know like 2 AM in the morning on a Saturday night. The only problem was, I had no idea what the show was going to be about. But really why should that stop me.

There was a radio disc jockey in Virginia Beach, that was sort of legendary in that area. He went by the name Henry the Bull, his real name was Henry Del Toro. And he had to be without a doubt, the first real shock jock in that area. I mean this guy did stuff on the radio that to this day are still talked about. Example, there's a place in Virginia Beach that is called Mount Trashmor. The reason for that is at one time it was a huge garbage dump, and after years and years of dumping garbage there, it formed a mountain. Well they covered the mountain with dirt and grass and made a park out of it.

So one time in the morning while Henry was on the air, he announced to the public, that because of a propane gas buildup at Mount Trashmor, the city was ordering an evacuation, because there was a danger of Mount Trashmor blowing up. That announcement by Henry, cause a huge traffic jam when an estimated 9000 people attempted to evacuate Virginia Beach. I mean it was pandemonium, people were going crazy trying to get off the beach. Well after about an hour of this, Henry announced to the audience that it was his April fools joke, and to this day people still talk about what he did that morning on the air.

Okay, so what does all of this have to do with me having a late-night television show? Well, while I am attempting to plan this TV show in my head I get a call from Henry Del Toro, who by the way I had never met. Henry was suggesting that myself and him do something in the media. Well the timing couldn't have been more perfect, I immediately told him about my idea for a late-night television show. The only problem was, I had no idea what the hell the show was going to be about. So anyway, me and Henry agreed to meet, to discuss how we were going to pull this off.

So after about two weeks of trying to get our schedules together in order to have a meeting, we met at a local restaurant for lunch. Like I said before, I had never met Henry, but listen to him often on the radio. I was shocked to see how withdrawn he was, I mean almost to the point of being very quiet and shy, nothing at all like his character on the radio he portrayed as the crazy shock jock Henry the Bull.

That all being said, we started to discuss

what the show was going to be about, an after a two hour lunch, and discussion, we came up with nothing. Finally Henry said, "let's just turn the camera on, and do whatever comes to mind". That's right, no rehearsal, no planning, we just have the camera follow us around and whatever happens happens. So I guess you could look back at it now and say, this in reality was actually the first reality show. But I thought what the hell let's give it a shot, and he and I had bought the time from the station, and it was $350 for a half hour spot, and I figured either way you looked at it, that was a half-hour commercial for the studio, and it was on the Fox affiliate, that reached close to 1 million people.

So I called in a friend of mine, Blake Marean to run the camera, because Blake had did that when I was on tour, and knew how to get a shot. I also called in one of our studio guitar players at the time name Larry, who in reality was an egomaniac and pictured himself as the reincarnated Rod Stewart, although Rod had not died yet.

So we set up a night in the studio to shoot the first show, with no idea what the hell we were going to do, but I knew that I was going to promote the studio to make it all worthwhile.

So there we are, me Henry and Larry in the studio, and I tell Blake, "okay turn the camera on", and I was going to start to show off by introducing myself, Larry, and Henry, but before I could get four words out of my mouth, for some reason the minute Henry saw the red light go on on the camera, he went from being this shy withdrawn guy, to a raving maniac. I mean he went from Henry Del Toro, to the character Henry the Bull, and the whole half hour consisted of trying to corral Henry, who was going off on everything in every direction possible. Nothing was off limits, and I thought to myself at that time, how the hell are we going to get this thing on the air. I mean the word controversial was not even close to describe, what was going on during that half-hour.

Well in short, the show aired at 2 AM on the Fox affiliate, and believe it or not it was a huge success. And looking back at it now, really it was 2 AM on a Saturday night, most of our audience were half drunk at the time, coming home from the clubs, so really, what did you expect, a highly educated television show.

I can remember when we ran out of

material to do, we actually did a segment, where me and Henry would look into the camera, and pretend that we were looking at something, saying to each other, "what is that, what the hell is that" and we would do that for like three minutes. Finally that became a major part of the show called, what the hell is that". We actually had a contest where we would give away $250 to anyone who could guess what we were looking at. In reality, there was nothing, we were just looking at the camera, and after nine weeks of running the contest, someone actually guessed the camera, and won the $250, but hey we ran that bit for 10 straight weeks, so the 250 was well worth it.

We wound up doing the show for a little over two years, and we would go to different locations, and do absolutely nothing but act like idiots, but we would involve people at the places we went and the show kept growing in popularity.

You remember I told you that we started on one station, a Fox affiliate that was locally based. However, at the end of two years, we were on 11 different cable networks, and, they were paying us for each episode of the show. Kind of mind-boggling wasn't it, here is a television show about nothing, and people in 11 different states are tuning in religiously watching this bullshit.

Well that all came to a tragic end one night, because you see Henry had a demon he was fighting, and that demon was prescription drugs.

I remember it like it was yesterday, we were supposed to shoot three shows in one day on a Wednesday, and I was over at Henry's apartment the night before. He was in pretty bad shape and had did a little more Percodan's then he should have. I remember him laying down, and me telling him, "Henry you have to get this shit under control, the shit is gonna kill your ass. I left that night at 2 AM, and said I would meet him at the studio the next day at 11. Henry usually showed up a half hour to 45 minutes early, so when it got to 10:45 that morning and Henry didn't show up, I started calling his apartment. I called it for probably an hour to an hour and a half, and he never answered the phone, so I sent everybody home who was involved with shooting the show, and at around 1 o'clock in the afternoon, I got a call from Henry's mother, informing me that Henry had been found dead that morning, still in bed, still fully dressed as I had left him.

I lost a good friend that night, but a friend that the public never really got to know. Yes he was funny, but it was a tortured humor, and the Henry the Bull character he portrayed so brilliantly, was in fact his escape from reality, which led him to his final escape, his death.

I did one more show, and had invited many of the people that were involved with the show as guests with Henry and myself. It was more or less a tribute to a passing friend. After that last show there was no way that I could continue doing it. So it ended, but as in life, with every loss, there is a gain. Life is for the living, and in my life, the beat goes on.

(Left To Right) Blake, Doc, Larry and Henry

Doc and Henry during the show

Well, I guess you have all figured out by now, that I got a little bored with what ever I was doing at the time, and with who ever I was doing it with after a while. That also went for the 6 X wives too. I know, I know, but hey, that was my problem I had to deal with on a daily basis, and actually still deal with it today. The only thing that never bored me was the music. I never got tired of that and probably never will. I believe making music is my reason for living.

So I guess it's time to get on with more stories. Now get this I'm on tour, and although the nights playing music are exciting and fulfilling, the daytime is getting boring. I mean how many times can you play golf, tennis, or go shopping. I guess if your normal person, which I am not, you could probably do that forever.

I get booked in a place call Winter Haven Florida, which is the home of a world-famous water ski show, at a place called, Cypress Gardens. One day we do something different, we go see this water ski show, which I might add was very good, and after the show I got to meet a bunch of the skiers, and the guys that drove the ski boats. While we were talking, they mentioned a new thing at the time, that they were putting in the show called para sailing. This is when they pulled, a person strapped into a parachute behind one of the ski boats, and it went up in the air, and as they swung him around to the beach, the guy strapped into the parachute, pulled the thing called a quick release, and he would slowly float down to the beach in front of the crowd.

Well, this really caught my interest, and I watched them do it one day at rehearsal. I mean what better way to skydive, then do it this way. The parachute is already open, and all you do is pull that quick release, and you float down to the ground.

We are booked in this club that we were working at for three weeks, and before you know it, the next thing I do, is go out and buy one of these speedboats, that cost $29,000, and of course a trailer to pull it around, and, a parachute, harness and a rope to pull it. Not just any rope, I had one made that was 5000 feet long, because I wanted to fly 1 mile high. Everybody at the show thought I was crazy, because their tow ropes they were using were only 1200 feet long. They had never heard of anyone pulling a parachute with a 5000 foot long tow rope. But I had made up my mind, I was going to do this, and I was going 5000 feet up in the air.

So we set the day to do it on a Sunday, because that was our off day from performing. The only problem was, we couldn't do it in Cypress Gardens, because the lakes that they had done the show on, was not more than a half a mile long at best, and that wouldn't give us enough space for a 5000 foot long tow rope to be run out. So we headed to the Gulf of Mexico in a place called Naples Florida, and I had four of the guys that drove the speedboats at Cypress Gardens go with us, because I mean really, these guys knew what they were doing, and me, I didn't know shit.

We hit Naples Florida, unloaded the boat on a public boat ramp that was nearby, and one of the guys drove the boat to the beach area, (that was deserted by the way), and we drove our car to the spot where we were going to meet them. Oh, by the way, did I tell you it was extremely windy that day, and all the guys from the park advised me not to do it in that much wind, because when you launch a guy in the parachute, he usually had to run a few steps until the shoot filled with air, and then it would take off. So this would be a first for many things that was all wrong that day. One, we were launching in 20 mile an hour winds, Two, we have 5000 feet of rope, and no one in our whole group, including the professionals, had no idea how that was going to work out or if it was even possible.

Well, we hook up the rope to the boat

and the driver slowly starts to pull away from the beach, and as a rope was going out, the boat is getting smaller and smaller, you could barely see it. So they strapped me into the parachute, and hooked the rope to the front of my harness. Problem number one, there is so much wind blowing, and the parachute is fully inflated and trying to fly on its own. Problem number two, the rope is in the water however there is so much slack in it because of the weight of the rope, that there is no way for the boat to pull the rope tight, in order to launch me in the parachute. It was now, that they all wanted to cancel the whole thing, and of course me and my brilliant wisdom, told everybody just grab a hold of me, and hold me down and back, while they eased the boat out, to get the slack out of the rope.

Well that sort of worked, but we couldn't get all of the slack out, but I said fuck it, tell them to nail it, and I'll run forward with the bitch, until the rope is out of the water.

So here they are holding me down, the parachute is trying to fly on its own, because of the wind, they are flooring the boat to get enough speed so I can launch, and all of a sudden that rope caught and yank me off my feet and forward. But like I said that parachute was completely inflated, so I shot straight up like a rocket ship, and once I got up there it was the most eerie feeling I have ever felt.

I mean you couldn't hear anything but the wind, you couldn't hear the boat, the people on the beach, nothing just the wind blowing in your ears, and as you look down at the boat that was towing me, it was about as big as my thumbnail, and believe it or not I was right over top of him. But that wind, rather than pulling me behind the boat, was filling up the parachute and it was trying to fly on its own. Once I looked down, it scared the shit out of me.

It was then that I decided, to pull the quick release, which disengaged the rope from my harness, and now I was floating down towards the water. I finally hit the water, and they picked me up in the boat, and brought me back to the beach. Bottom line was I did it, but I will tell you now, after all that money I invested in the boat and gear, I never did it again.

Doc, Getting Ready To Launch, And They Are Trying To Hold Him Down, Because The Wind Was So Strong That Day, That The Parachute Was Lifting Doc Off The Ground

During the many years that I spent as a touring musician, the last 12 years on tour, I spent traveling with my dog. His name was Fred, and he was an 85 pound black chow chow. Anybody that knows me, knows I am a devout animal lover, and Fred was my best friend.

I will admit that on occasions, traveling with a dog did pose some problems. Like when we were doing the Texas tour, I would not allow him to be put in a cage, and fly in the baggage department, so I wound up hiring a private plane, so Fred could fly in the seat next to me.

There were other incidences when my buddy Fred caused a problem. One of the main ones, was some of the hotels that we were booked in, did not allow pets. And I had a standard rule, if Fred couldn't stay, then neither would I. It was always stated in my performance rider, that if the hotel did not allow pets, then they would have to book me in another room in a different hotel, that would allow Fred to be in the room.

I remember one time, we were booked into Caesars Palace in Las Vegas, and we pulled up to the hotel, and I told my wife Judy, to take Fred inside and get him into the room. Well she made it as far as the lobby, and of course Fred was pulling her all over the place. Just then one of the front desk clerks, rushed up to her and said "Madame, we do not allow pets in Caesar's Palace". My wife responded, "this is Doc Holiday's dog", figuring they were aware of the performance rider, that stated my dog had to stay with me in the hotel. The front desk clerk responded by saying, "I don't care who's dog it is, we don't allow pets at Caesars Palace".

My wife came back out to our bus, and told me they would not allow Fred in the hotel. Well, you can imagine after doing a 17 Hour drive to get there, I was in no mood for this bullshit. So I got a hold of Fred's leash, and me, and my wife, and Fred walked back into the lobby. Well I didn't get 15 feet into the lobby, and out comes this front desk clerk ass hole, running at me like it was the end of the fuckin' world. Of course Fred, saw it as an attack, and immediately went after him.

So here I am, holding back at 85 pound chow chow, and this fucking moron is yelling at me, to get my dog out of the lobby. Well I got my wife, to walk Fred outside to our tour bus, and I asked the front desk jerk off, "let me speak to your manager".

The manager came out in a matter of moments, and I explained to him who I was, and that we were performing that night in the show room, (and by the way it was sold out). I also explained to him, that in our performance rider, it clearly stated, that if the hotel did not allow pets, then they would have to supply me with a room of equal quality, nearby, that did allow pets. His response, was that they were not aware of that, nor could he do anything about it. My response to him was, "well you two ass holes, better get on that fucking stage tonight, return all the money for the tickets you sold to the show, because I'm not going on".

Just then, the hotel manager, came out with the talent buyer and the promoter, and told me to calm down, they will straighten this all out.

So in short, we played Caesar's Palace that night to a sold-out crowd, and I have, framed on my wall, the contract for that job. And it states, "for this performance, Fred, will be considered a member of the band and allowed on the property at all times".

You know Fred was a different kind of dog, I mean he was raise different than most dogs. He spent every day of his life either in a tour bus or a motel room. I can't remember when he ever ran free, except when he was in the motel room or the bus, then he never was on a leash, ever.

He was a great dog, and he was never house trained, but he also never went to the bathroom in the bus or any of the motel rooms. He would always tell you when he had to go out, and at that point we would put his leash on him, and most of the time my wife would walk him.

I can remember one time, we were in Fort Lauderdale Florida, and a funny thing, every time Fred would come into a motel room, he would lay on top of the air conditioner, and most of them were near a window, so he would have the cold air blowing on him, and be able to look out the window at the same time. Well, getting back to Fort Lauderdale, Fred had a serious ear condition, and I brought him to the vet. This vet informed me, that the ear infection was cancerous, and he advised me to have Fred, at age 9, put asleep. He said that the infection was so bad it had spread throughout his head and neck, and also the average lifespan of a chow chow that large was only nine years old anyway, and Fred had reached that age. Well, there was no way I was buying that horse shit. I took him to another vet for a second opinion. That vet told me that there were antibiotics that could fight that infection, however they were extremely expensive, and he suggested that Fred be hospitalized for at least six weeks. He also stated that he saw no cancer in him whatsoever, just the severe infection that he had that was rooted in his ear, and that infection was quite common in chow chow's.

So I elected to follow his direction, and me and my wife started to care for Fred while we were on the road. Every town we went in, we brought him to a local vet to monitor his progress. And sure enough he was progressing. At the end of 10 weeks of treatment, and a little over $4000 in vet bills, and antibiotics, Fred showed no signs of the infection whatsoever, and he was back to his normal self.

A very strange thing with Fred, doing his whole life he never ate dog food of any kind. Myself while on tour would never eat in a restaurant, me and my wife always got room service, and no matter what we were having for dinner, Fred had the same dinner. We were eating prime rib, mashed potatoes, a vegetable, salad, and cheesecake for dessert. That's what Fred ate, and the only time he ever got sick was that time in Fort Lauderdale with the ear infection.

I can remember one time we played a club in Mobile, Alabama, called Jarrods, and of course it was always in my performance rider, that all my meals were included in the engagement, along with my wife's, and like I said earlier, we never ate in the restaurant, it was always room service.

Well one day the owner of the hotel and club, a guy called, Prentice Moore, was talking to the general manager, Bill, and said, "damn, that Doc and his wife eat a lot of food, there getting three orders of breakfasts, lunch and three dinners every day". Bill said,, "no Doc is only eating one, his wife is eating one, and Fred is eating one.

I was called down to the office, and Prentice had told me, that we were on our way to breaking the club record for weekly sales, and he was kind of congratulating me on that accomplishment. But then he turned and looked at me, and in a strong southern accent said, "but damn Doc, do we have to feed the dog to". He had a smile on his face when he said it, and I said Prentice, "the dog goes, and I go, and that means you don't break your record". We both had a small laugh, and yes we did break the club record that week.

Well about five years later, I quit touring, and Fred and my wife finally had a house that we were living in, and this would be the first house in Fred's life that he had ever witness staying in. And I will tell you right now he didn't like it. I mean he was just not himself, he wasn't as energetic as he normally was, in he just didn't seem happy at all. Then one day when he was just turning 16, he developed a slight cough, and of course I took him right to a vet. The vet told me that it would probably just a small cold. So I took Fred home and waited for the cold to run its course as the vet had instructed me.

Well we got a call, that we had to make a trip, from Virginia to Canada, to visit one of my wife's relatives. So I bought a motor home for the trip, and of course Fred was going with us, and I tell you it was like he was reborn, he was back on the road and loving it., But he still had that cough, it seemed to be getting worse, and it got worse every time he would have to exert any kind of energy.

Well we arrived in Canada, checked into a motel room, and of course Fred headed right for the air conditioner, and jumped on top of it. It was plain to see he was back in his element.

After being in the motel room for about seven hours, I noticed that Fred had gotten off of the air conditioner, and I said to my wife, you better take Fred out, he probably have to go to the bathroom. She went into the bathroom to put the leash on him, and she screamed for me to come in there, and there was Fred laying on the floor unresponsive.

I went crazy, I yelled at her to call that vet that was about 300 feet away from where we were staying. I picked Fred up, and his body was limp, and I carried him that 300 feet, and the vet let us right in, as I laid him on the table, and the vet told me he was gone.

We later found out, that he was misdiagnosed, and had a heart condition, that could have been treated, however, we were not told that in Virginia, we were told he had a slight cold.

Fred lived to be 16 years old, an unbelievable long time for an 85 pound chow chow. That incident broke my heart, and I still feel the pain of losing my best friend. I buried Fred in Nova Scotia Canada, on the island that we lived on, and to this day his grave is still visible and kept up by a caretaker every week.

When my buddy, Fred, crossed over the rainbow bridge, he took a big part of me with him, and hopefully I will see my friend again. You know, As a footnote here, veterinarians should be held up to the same standards that doctors who treat humans, that are held up to, but unfortunately they are not. To me Fred was a child, my child, and if any doctor of humans were to make that mistake, that vet made on Fred, and that may have been the reason he passed away, there would be serious charges brought against that Doctor. However humanity does not look at it that way, when it comes to a veterinarian, and that my friends, is wrong, and will never be right.

Doc And Fred Before A Performance

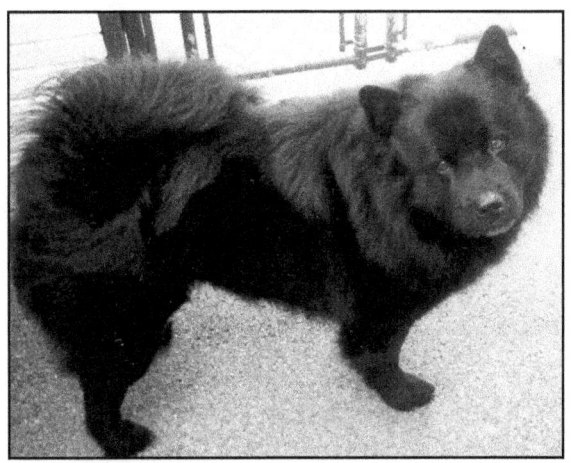

Fred, Knowing Doc Was Going To Work

Fred's Grave Today In Nova Scotia, Canada

My Final Goodbye (Maybe)

Well, it looks like we've reached the end of this part of the journey, but then again maybe not. Because all the stories that hopefully you have just read, are really just the tip of the iceberg, when it comes to my life's story. But now that my health has really taken a downward spiral, I felt it really necessary to get some of these things in print, so they are not lost forever, or changed, by being told by a second party after my death and watered down.

During my life I made some good business decisions, but on the personal side I made some horribly bad decisions. So it amazes me every day, why am the last one standing, or at least one of the last ones standing.

I guess because of all my health problems, in a way, I'm kind of paying for my misspent youth. Which ever the case may be, I must be still here on this earth, to do something important. Maybe this book is one of those things.

It's hard to look back and realize that only four years ago, I was running around, playing golf and tennis, partying day and night, without a care in the world. Then from out of nowhere, my body started to deteriorate. First it was a slight pain in my back, then my legs, then diagnosed with diabetes, high blood pressure and deterioration of my knees and hips. To put it bluntly, my body was breaking. But that being said, my mind and my ears were still working at 100%. So all they really have to do, with just get me to a recording studio, where I could do what was known as in the business, Doc Holiday's FM Music, (FUCKIN' MAGIC). Once there, everything is working at full capacity, and I might add still working today, better than ever.

In the past two years, I have probably made and produced, some of the best records I have ever made in my whole career. And even as I'm writing this book, for some strange reason it gets even better and better every session.

The music business has changed dramatically over the years, and for some unknown reason, I was able to change with it, but still maintain the history and integrity of all the early music that came before me, and at the start of my career in the early 50s.

Maybe that's what gives me an edge, in producing today. I'm able to reach back into the past of my career, and pull out different sounds and techniques that were used in the making of that music in that point of time, and fuse them into today's sound, and by doing that create something really unique. I mean, when you listen to my productions today, there are certain little parts hidden in the music, that subliminally, your ears are relating too. It's hard to really figure it out, but those parts are in that production. And the bottom line is. It works.

But let's not forget the artist. Many of them were brilliant, some made it, and some did not. But that doesn't take away from their skill, and their artistry, and their ability, to create a historical piece of music that will live on long after they are gone. You see I truly believe, after doing this for 60+ years, that making it in the entertainment industry is 70% skill, and 30% luck. That's right, you heard me correct, 30% luck.

So the best advice I can give anyone entering the entertainment business, with a dream of becoming a star, and leaving a legacy, is simple. Keep riding that Bitch, until the wheels fall off, never give up. You cannot hit the bull's-eye unless you're throwing darts. The day you quit trying, is the day you fail, if you quit trying, you really didn't deserve it to begin with. Persistence wears down resistance, and that not only pertains to the music industry, but in everything you do in life. I know because it happened to me, but 1 never gave up, and refused to give up to this day. I could see myself now on my deathbed saying my last words. A simple thank you to my wife Judy for caring for me these last four years, for my daughter Carmela for not making the mistakes that I made, for my late daughter Michele for trying to figure it all out, and never quite got the right answers, and left me way to early. And the last words out of my mouth will be, Bobby raise that guitar volume in that part, Dale is playing a cool lick there. And "WHEW", "What a fuckin' ride that was"

Below are just a few of the Artists that I have had the honor of working with that made musical history, some made it, and some did not make it to the top, BUT THEY ALL MADE MUSICAL HISTORY AND THAT'S WHAT REALLY COUNTS IN THE END.

www.ingramcontent.com/pod-product-compliance
Lightning Source LLC
Chambersburg PA
CBHW060338170426
43202CB00014B/2813